Songs My Grandma Sang

MICHAEL B. CURRY

Songs My Grandma Sang

MICHAEL B. CURRY

Morehouse Publishing
NEW YORK · HARRISBURG · DENVER

Morehouse Publishing, 19 East 34th Street, New York, NY 10016
Morehouse Publishing is an imprint of Church Publishing Incorporated.

www.churchpublishing.org

Cover image: Photo of Nellie Royster Strayhorne, Bishop Michael Curry's maternal grandmother.

Cover design by Laurie Klein Westhafer
Typeset by Denise Hoff

Library of Congress Cataloging-in-Publication Data

Curry, Michael B.

    Songs my grandma sang / Michael B. Curry.

        pages cm

    Includes bibliographical references.

    ISBN 978–0–8192–2993–9 (pbk.)—ISBN 978–0–8192–2994–6 (ebook)   1. Curry, Michael B.—Songs and music.   2. Music, Influence of.   3. African American Episcopalians—North Carolina—Biography.   I. Title.

    BX5995.C785A3 2015

    264'.23—dc23   2015002688

Printed in the United States of America

Contents

Foreword by J. Neil Alexander   vii

CHAPTER 1:   The Songs of Many Grandmothers   1

CHAPTER 2:   Why Jesus   12

CHAPTER 3:   Go Tell It on the Mountain   25

CHAPTER 4:   Episcopalians—Witnesses?   35

CHAPTER 5:   Jesus's Family Values   45

CHAPTER 6:   Glory!   59

CHAPTER 7:   A Song Seldom Sung   70

CHAPTER 8:   Ride On!   86

CHAPTER 9:   How to Know When the Spirit is in Your Church   99

CHAPTER 10:   Who'll Be a Witness?   114

CHAPTER 11:   Keep Going!   124

a bird doesn't sing because
it has an answer, it sings
because it has a song.

From "A Cup of Sun"
by Joan Walsh Anglund
a favorite quote of the
late Maya Angelou

Foreword

When my children were small we lived in New York City, and a regular feature of those beautiful summer evenings was a subway ride away at Yankee Stadium. We would grab some cheap seats and not-so-cheap eats and delight in watching our Yankees, win or lose. We would watch our left-handed sluggers put home run after home run in the seats of the short porch in right field. We would come out of our seats when our boys of summer pulled off a suicide squeeze. The infielders in those days were so good that one could easily forget you were at a ballgame and not the ballet. My children knew every player, the number on every jersey, and could follow baseball statistics before they understood basic math. Those were memorable summer nights brimming with the sort of stuff from which a good life is made.

Eddie Layton, the only man in history to play for the Yankees, the Knicks, and the

Rangers, was the stadium organist. He would work up the crowd with his prowess at the keyboard, get us singing and clapping, and offer a constant running commentary on the game from the console of his Hammond B-3. No matter what was happening on the field, opening day or game seven of the world series, the experience would not have been all that it was without the deep, intuitive understanding of baseball, and New York fans, that flowed from Eddie Layton's fingers.

But there is more. At every single game—at the last crack of the bat, the final pop of a fielder's glove—someone in the sound booth would hit the switch and crank up the volume and everyone in the stadium, and well beyond it, could hear Ol' Blue Eyes begin the closing hymn of every game: *Start spreading the news!* Win or lose, victory or defeat, we had some news and we were going to tell it. You always left Yankee Stadium singing along with the Chairman of the Board.

When you think of Bishop Michael Curry, I don't suspect baseball is the first thing that comes to mind. I suspect it is his preaching. But there is a deep connection here. Bishop Michael is a renowned preacher in The Episcopal Church and well beyond. The power of the

Word of God to instruct and inform, the transformational energy at the heart of the Gospel of Jesus, and the sheer power of the Holy Spirit to change lives and alter the status quo, are the dangerous, potentially explosive assets in his arsenal. When Bishop Michael preaches you expect to be instructed, inspired, propelled, and sent. Bishop Michael is blessed with the gifts to deliver strong word on Word. Listening to Bishop Michael preach the gospel is a lot like hearing Eddie Layton weave a summer night's baseball game into an unforgettable, formative, glimpse of something beyond ourselves. This is important. Important because in what follows, Bishop Michael lets us in on a secret: *no one ever went home from church whistling the sermon!*

Christians sing. And the songs of the church, like the Psalms for Israel, are the most penetrating source of the church's prayer and the most accurate indication of what is close to the hearts of God's people.

As a pastor I am secretly delighted when I visit with a family at the death of a loved one. I will sometimes ask, "What was your moma's favorite scripture or psalm? Perhaps that will give us a place to start in thinking about her burial service." And one of the children would pipe up with, "Moma's favorite psalm was *I want to walk as a child of the light.*" Or, "Moma's favorite story from the Bible was the part where they *Crown Him with Many Crowns.*" Or, "When Moma was unhappy or depressed, she would always read that part in the Bible about the *Amazing Grace that saved a wretch like her.*" Why is this so? Because when the chips are down we turn to those texts and tunes that have bored their way into our souls, that live in the deep recesses of our consciousness, and that provide healing balm like nothing else.

For me, when life is challenging and full of trouble, the words of Holy Scripture and the prayers of the church are great gifts, but nothing wells up with salvation's healing salve quite like the hymns and spiritual songs that are way down deep. The book you are about to read is Michael Curry's personal witness to the truth that Christians sing, and what Christians sing may tell you more about what is really important to them than anything they could tell you.

I doubt it was Bishop Michael's first concern when he penned these pages, but this book should also be read as a provocative reminder of how important it is to teach our children and young people the songs and hymns, the spiritual food of the faith. And here I am not talking about junk food. I'm not talking about the little choruses that might well have their place around the campfire at summer camp. I am talking about the rich deposit of the church's faith that is stored in the church's hymnals and songbooks, the songs we sing in the wilderness, the hymns that guide our journeys, the texts that travel with us all our days. God's people are a singing people and if our children are going to have faith, they are going to have to learn to sing their great grandmother's songs of faith.

J. Neil Alexander
Lent 2015
Sewanee

CHAPTER 1

The Songs of Many Grandmothers

Tom Brokaw's 1998 book *The Greatest Generation* told the story of a generation of people in the United States who were raised in the hard times of the Great Depression only to go off to fight the Second World War, essentially saving human civilization from the dark nightmare of fascism, racism, and nationalized hatred. After the war they came home and rebuilt the country. He was right to speak of them as "the greatest generation."

But there was another, just before the greatest one. They were the people who gave birth to and raised "the greatest generation" through the breadlines and in the dust bowl that was the Great Depression. It was from them that "the greatest generation" learned the faith and the values that made them who they became.

This was the world of my grandparents on both sides of my family. They were all the grandchildren of former slaves in Alabama and North Carolina. Like the stories told in Isabel Wilkerson's *The Warmth of Other Suns,* they, along with many others significantly defined by sharecropping and segregation, migrated from the rural south to the urban north in hope of finding new possibilities of freedom for themselves and their progeny. From their grandparents, who were themselves once in bondage, they learned the spirituals created by fellow slaves. They gleaned stories and sayings whose wisdom had been tried in the fire of this hard life. As they grew up, they learned songs descended from the spirituals, later called gospel. When they weren't in church sometimes they sang the blues and rocked to jazz, which came into being in their world and time.

Their songs and sayings reflected a deep faith and profound wisdom that taught them how to shout "glory" while cooking in "sorrow's kitchen," as they used to say. In this there was a hidden treasure that saw many of them through, and that is now a spiritual inheritance for those of us who have come after them. That treasure was a sung faith expressing a way of being in relationship with the living God of Jesus that was real, energizing, sustaining, loving, liberating, and life-giving.

In September of 1930 Dietrich Bonhoeffer, a brilliant young German theologian, came to America to study at Union Seminary in New York. Today he is rightly seen as one of the greatest theologians of the twentieth century and one of the holy martyrs of the church for his sacrifice in radical obedience to Jesus and his Gospel way. His following the way of Jesus led him to participate in the opposition to the tyranny of Adolf Hitler and his Nazi ideology and state. For that Bonhoeffer was executed on April 9, 1945. But in September of 1930 Bonhoeffer was a student coming to New York's Union Seminary to study. Alongside his reading and writing he would become friends and spend time with an African American seminarian named Franklin Fisher from Birmingham, Alabama.

Fisher would take his young German friend with him to Abyssinian Baptist Church in Harlem. There Bonhoeffer encountered an expression of Christianity he had never known. There he encountered the generation of my grandparents. There he heard preaching that lifted souls wearied by work weeks devoid of much to "Mount Pisgah's lofty heights" to behold, as Moses did, a promised land. He came to know people who strangely commingled joy and laughter while cooking "in sorrow's kitchen." There he heard and saw Dr. Adam Clayton Powell, Sr. preach powerfully and witness fervently to a Gospel of Jesus that was at once deeply personal, pervasively communal, and pointedly political. He encountered the evangelical and social Gospel incarnated in the nitty-gritty of life, in lived faith.

But it was the songs—the singing—that captured it all for him. Charles Marsh in his incredible book on Bonhoeffer, *Strange Glory*, observes that while we know how profoundly Bonhoeffer was affected by this experience, the usually reflective and analytical Bonhoeffer "never wrote an account of Sunday mornings at Abyssinian."[1] Professor Marsh points to one explanation offered by another scholar, Ruth

1. Charles Marsh, *Strange Glory: A Life of Dietrich Bonheoffer* (New York: Alfred A. Knopf, 2014), 119.

Zellar, who said, "that black worship, particularly in song, was so overwhelming and personal for [Bonhoeffer] that he found it difficult to analyze in writing."[2]

He heard singing of spirituals, the sorrow songs and the glory songs, created in Nebuchadnezzar's fiery furnace of chattel slavery and yet yielding not dross but precious metal, to feed the soul. He heard the songs of gospel, the musical descendants of the spirituals and the blues. He heard them sing songs with words like these:

> Sometimes I feel discouraged,
> And think my life in vain,
> But then the Holy Spirit
> Revives my soul again.
> There is a balm in Gilead
> To make the wounded whole,
> There is a balm in Gilead,
> To heal the sin sick soul.[3]
>
> I want Jesus to walk with me,
> In my joys and in my sorrow,
> I want Jesus to walk with me.[4]

---

2. *Ibid.*
3. *LEVAS II,* #203.
4. *LEVAS II,* #70.

What a friend we have in Jesus
All our sins and griefs to bear[5]

Precious Lord, take my hand
lead me on, let me stand
I am tired, I am weak I am worn
Through the storm, through the night
Lead me on, through the night
Take my hand, precious Lord
And lead me home [6]

Blessed assurance, Jesus is mine.
O what a foretaste of glory divine.
Heir of salvation, purchased of God
Born of his Spirit, washed in his
   blood.
This is my story, this is my song,
Praising my Savior all the day long.
This is my story, this is my song,
Praising my Savior all the day long.[7]

Through these songs and the worship of
Almighty God that they inspired and were a part
of, he beheld the vision of a kingdom not made or
controlled by this world or any of its purported
powers. He heard of a justice not compromised

---

5. *LEVAS II*, #109.
6. *LEVAS II*, #106.
7. *LEVAS II*, #184.

by any culture, of the love of Jesus that is a "balm in Gilead," and of a freedom worth fighting for. Through these songs he felt what Doris Ackers's gospel song called a "sweet, sweet Spirit," that clearly was "the Spirit of the Lord."[8] The experience of the living God of Jesus that these songs reflected would feed him in a prison cell when, like the Israelites exiled in Babylon or Paul and Silas singing in a Roman jail or Martin King writing "A Letter from a Birmingham Jail," he would have to sing "the Lord's song in a strange land."[9] There is spiritual power and wisdom in these songs. These songs, reflecting and facilitating an intimate and yet communal experience of God, that so deeply affected Dietrich Bonhoeffer were the songs of my grandmother.

They were not just songs with catchy tunes. They were songs that sang of a way of viewing the world that could make life livable no matter what. They reflected a way of looking at life, a way of engaging life, a way of dealing with whatever life threw at you in faith and hope.

> Be not dismayed, what'er betide.
> God will take care of you.[10]

---

8. *LEVAS II*, #120.
9. Psalm 137 and Acts 16.
10. *LEVAS II*, #183.

Why should I feel discouraged.
His eye is on the sparrow,
And I know he watches me.
I sing because I'm happy.
I sing because I'm free
His eye is on the sparrow,
And I know he watches me.[11]

But these were not merely songs of individual piety. These songs sang of a new world. They sang of a liberation and salvation in this life, and in the life with God beyond this life. They were songs that sang of divine justice that could not be twisted or compromised by human sin. These songs sang of Jesus who could steady "the weary traveler." They reflected a way to "set the captive free."

Didn't my Lord deliver Daniel,
So why not every man.[12]

Oh, freedom! Oh, freedom!
Oh freedom over me!
An' befo' I'd be a slave
I'll be buried in my grave
An' go home to my Lord an' be free.[13]

---

11. *LEVAS II*, #191.
12. *LEVAS II*, #182.
13. *LEVAS II*, #225.

They are songs of wit and wisdom, saturated with the "weight of glory." These were the songs of Nellie Strayhorn, my maternal grandmother, from whom I learned them as a child sitting in the kitchen while she cooked, told stories, and hummed or sang. It was her lively, uncompromised, vibrant faith in God that has shaped my deeper level of faith and theological world view. Hers was a faith that really believed that, "He's got the whole world in his hands."[14]

My sister and I became particularly close to her as children, when our mother—her daughter—Dorothy became sick for a long period of time and eventually died. This woman, then in her late seventies with cane always in hand, grabbed that cane, sang her songs, praised the Lord, told stories of old North Carolina, and helped our father rear some more children, singing all along,

> I'm so glad Jesus lifted me.
> I'm so glad, Jesus lifted me.
> I'm so glad Jesus lifted me
> Singing glory, hallelujah,
> Jesus lifted me.[15]

---

14. *LEVAS II*, #217.
15. *LEVAS II*, #105.

Not too many years before she died I went to visit her. While I was there, she and her best friend, Mrs. Clara King, decided that they wanted to go to the store, so I drove them. Because of construction work, we had to park across the street. The three of us got out of the car. The two of them, well up in their eighties, with canes in their hands, were on either side of me, holding on to my arms. We were a sight to see. We walked very slowly across the street, longer than the changed light actually allowed, but the traffic saw who we were and cars waited patiently for us to cross. When we finally arrived on the other side of the street, they slowed and stopped. No one said a word, but I could feel the pressure on my arms as they struggled through arthritis and the hardness of life to step up on the curb. When they both succeeded, Aunt Clara said to grandma, "We've got a good God, don't we, Stray." (Grandma's married name was Strayhorne, but Aunt Clara always called her "Stray.") A brief chorus of *amens* ensued and then they started to sing.

> Then sings my soul
> My Savior God to thee.
> How great thou art,
> How great thou art.

> Then sings my soul,
> My Savior God to thee.
> How great thou art.
> How great thou art.[16]

To behold Spirit of the living God in a simple footstep is to know something about life that is worth knowing whether you are of "the greatest generation," the boomers, GenXers, millenials, or of a generation yet to be born. This may be the spiritual gift of my grandmother and her generation: simply living life with God, following in the way of Jesus, and singing their songs along the way.

---

16. *LEVAS II*, #60.

CHAPTER 2

Why Jesus

Join hands, disciples of the faith
What-e'er your race may be!
Who serves my Father as his child
Is surely kin to me

In Christ there is no East or West
In him no South or North
But one great fellowship of love
Throughout the whole wide earth.[17]

---

17. *The Hymnal 1982*, 529.

> An account of the genealogy of Jesus
> the Messiah, the son of David, the
> son of Abraham . . . (Matthew 1:1)

> Go therefore and make disciples
> of all nations, baptizing them in
> the name of the Father and of the
> Son and of the Holy Spirit, and
> teaching them to obey everything
> that I have commanded you.
> (Matthew 28:19, 20)

Jesus came to show us the way to become more
than we ever could, or would, be on our own.
Another way to say it is that God came among us
in the person of Jesus of Nazareth to show us the
way to be right and reconciled with the God who
created us all, and with each other as children
of that one God and Father of us all. In so doing
he has shown us the way to end what is often a
nightmare of human devising and the way to live
nothing less than God's very dream for us and
all creation. Let me show you what I mean. Do
not be offended by what I am about to say, but
the truth is that being a member of the human
race is not that much of an accomplishment.

It is easy to be of the human race. That
is really just biology. Being human is easy. It

is simply a matter of consumption, respiration and reproduction—breathing, eating, and making more of our kind. That is not much of an accomplishment! If the truth be told, we have two cats who can do that. Did not Jesus say, "Is not life more than food, and the body more than clothing? . . . Consider the lilies of the field, how they grow" (Matthew 6:25–28). "I have come that you may have life and have it abundantly" (John 10:10). Jesus came to show us the way to be more than just the human race. He came to show us the way to become the human family of God. In that is our hope and salvation, now and unto the day of eternity.

I must hasten to say that this is not really my idea. It is at the heart of the biblical story. Let me give you one example, from the Gospel according to Matthew. It is not an accident that Matthew begins his telling of the Jesus story with a genealogy and ends his Gospel with Jesus commissioning his followers to go into the world to create a new family of disciples born, not of blood, but of baptismal water, not a mere biological life and existence but a life defined and determined by the teachings and the ways of Jesus.

> An account of the genealogy of
> Jesus the Messiah, the son of
> David, the son of Abraham . . .
> (Matthew 1:1)
>
> Go therefore and make disciples
> of all nations, baptizing them in
> the name of the Father and of
> the Son and of the Holy Spirit,
> and teaching them to obey every-
> thing that I have commanded you.
> (Matthew 28:19, 20)

That is not an accident.

Consider the genealogy. There are two
genealogies of Jesus in the New Testament.
Genealogical research has become an avoca-
tion of my wife's. The amount of information about one's family and ancestry available
online is simply extraordinary. As a birthday
gift this year my daughters and I gave her the
ancestry.com DNA kit. I look forward to the
results to find out who I am really married to.
Regardless, this kind of genealogical and DNA
research is intended to glean biographical and
even biological facts and information about
one's family.

Genealogies in the Bible were not about authenticating one's biographical or biological inheritance. They were more about what one's life meant rather than the facts that made it up. So when two genealogies of the same person vary in details there is usually a message encoded in that, not a genetic error. Such is the case with the two genealogies of Jesus in Luke 3:23–38 and Matthew 1:1–17. Of particular note: Luke traces Jesus's ancestry to Adam, thus linking Jesus with the common history and ancestry of humanity, created in the image and likeness of God. Matthew, on the other hand traces Jesus's ancestry to Abraham. Again, that is not a contradiction; it is an encoded message. Matthew is trying to tell us something.

Go back to the early days of the Book of Genesis when Abraham (Abram) and Sarah (Sarai) first appear on the stage of the biblical story. One can image Abraham and Sarah in their old age living in the ancient equivalent of a retirement community. They are doing well. They are elders. In ancient and traditional cultures, old age is a blessing, to be honored and respected. It is the prime of life, not over the hill. So Abraham and Sarah are living well. Happy. Secure. Comfortable.

Then this word from the Lord.

Now the Lord said to Abram, "Go from your country and your kindred and your father's house to the land that I will show you. I will make of you a great nation, and I will bless you, and make your name great, so that you will be a blessing. I will bless those who bless you, and the one who curses you I will curse; and in you all the families of the earth shall be blessed." (Genesis 12:1–3)

They are sent away from all that they know: family, friends, community, blood ties, and kinfolk, to a land not their own, to a people not their own. There they are to become a new family, for through them, "all the families of the earth will be blessed." There is a message here. Religious faith is not intended to divide and fragment humanity. On the contrary, if it is God who is calling, it is meant to be a blessing, not a curse. Abraham, Sarah, and Hagar (who enters the story later) become the ancestors of three of the great religious faiths of the human family: Judaism, Christianity, and Islam.

Religion, faith, spirituality—call it what you will; if it is born of God, it is made for blessing—not curse, to show the way to love—not hate, to give life—not take it way, to enable—to beautify, to better, to improve, to restore, to renew, and to heal the creation as the Jewish tradition of *Tikkun olam* teaches us. Religion exists to bless. That is what Abraham was about. And Abraham is counted as an ancestor of Jesus, through whom the curse of sin, hatred and division, violence and bigotry, injustice and selfishness will be banished by the titanic power of blessing.

> No more let sins and sorrows grow,
> Nor thorns infest the ground;
> He comes to make his blessings flow
> Far as the curse is found,
> Far as, far as the curse is found.
>
> Joy to the world! the Lord is come;
> Let earth receive her King;
> Let every heart prepare him room,
> And heaven and nature sing,
> And heaven and nature sing,
> And heaven, and heaven and nature
>   sing.[18]

---

18. *The Hymnal 1982*, 100.

Tamar, Rahab, Ruth, Bathsheba

A genealogy is a family tree. The standard format for a first century Palestinian Jewish genealogy was to trace one's ancestry through the male line. Look at other genealogies in the Bible. They all trace ancestry via the patriarchal lineage.[19] That has long fascinated me because while genealogies trace via the male line, one is Jewish not by virtue of your father, but because of your mother. If your mother is Jewish, so are you. That was also the case in the first century, regardless of the patriarchal lineage traced on the genealogy. Matthew follows this convention. Then something happens. There is an interruption, a dissident note, a strange sound in the symphony. Contrary to convention, counter cultural to our assumptions, four women make rather dramatic appearances in Jesus's genealogy.

Biblical scholar Phyllis Trible once wrote a book about the painful stories of biblical women who had to struggle mightily against the odds stacked against them. These were

---

19. See, for example, Genesis 5:1f (Adam to Noah), Exodus 6:14 (the Genealogy of Moses and Aaron), Ruth 4:13 (King David), Nehemiah 7:5f (the exiles who returned from Babylon), Luke 3:23f (Jesus).

women who, because of social conventions and customs, were dealt a bad hand. Trible appropriately titled her book *Texts of Terror.* One of the women mentioned in Tamar, who is in Jesus's lineage. Her story is told in the thirty-eighth chapter of Genesis. Tamar was a woman who took a mess and made a miracle. By sheer "Mother Wit"—the street name for what the biblical tradition calls "Wisdom"—she found the way to life from the midst of social death. And Tamar was an ancestor of the Lord Jesus. Matthew is trying to tell us something.

The next woman who appears in the genealogy of Jesus is Rahab (Joshua 2 and 6). Now, to be sure, Rahab must be discussed rather delicately. She lived in the city of Jericho after the Hebrews had been set free from slavery in Egypt. She was a resident of Jericho when

Joshua fought the battle of Jericho.
Jericho. Jericho.
Joshua fought the battle of Jericho.
And the walls came tumbling down.[20]

Rahab was a business woman, though likely not in the ancient equivalent of the Chamber

---

20. *LEVAS II*, #223.

of Commerce. She was the Miss Kitty of the Old Testament. Miss Kitty was a character in one of my grandmother's favorite television shows, *Gunsmoke*. I used to watch it with her sometimes. It never occurred to me to ask what Miss Kitty actually did for a living. Oh, it was obvious that she was the owner of the saloon where everybody hung out. The full story of the business that she ran was not told, just assumed or implied. This was obviously not a twenty-first century show. It was the 1960s. Rahab, like Miss Kitty, ran a brothel. Yet for her courage in helping the Hebrews, she is honored as a heroine of Israel and an ancestor of Jesus.

Ruth's story is told in the book that bears her name. She and her mother-in-law, Naomi, find themselves widows, living in a land that is not of their families. When Naomi determines to return to her ancestral home, Ruth, the text says, "clings" to her. Ruth adopts Naomi's family as her own (the Spirit just dropped a hint here). Just listen to how Ruth gives voice to her decision to join the family of Naomi.

> But Ruth said,
> "Do not press me to leave you
> or to turn back from following you!

Where you go, I will go;
where you lodge, I will lodge;
your people shall be my people,
and your God my God.
Where you die, I will die—

there will I be buried.
May the Lord do thus and so to me,
and more as well,
if even death parts me from you."
(Ruth 1:16–17)

In time, after the exercise of some Mother Wit, Ruth marries into the Hebrew people through a man named Boaz and becomes the great grandmother of King David.

Alas, there is Bathsheba, who first appears in the eleventh chapter of 2 Samuel and remains a major player in the court of King David thereafter. A wife of David, mother of Solomon, Bathsheba was really the power behind the throne, engineering the establishment of her son as successor to David.

The inclusion of these women in the genealogy of Jesus is sending a clear message. First, they are all women. That, as we suggested earlier, is a major statement in itself in a first century Jewish genealogy. Second, each one through the skillful application of Mother Wit gleaned life on the edges of death and made hope happen against the odds. They are witnesses that the way of Jesus changes the way of the world. They are witnesses that in Jesus "things which were cast down are being raised up, and things which had grown old are being made new, and that all things are being brought to their perfection by him through whom all things were made. . . ."[21]

But third, every one of them—Tamar, Rahab, Ruth, and Bathsheba—was a gentile, a non-Jew. Tamar and Rahab were Canaanites, women of one of the peoples of Palestine. Ruth was a Moabite. Bathsheba was a Hittite. None of them was Jewish. The grandmother of David, Israel's greatest king, was not Jewish. These ancestors of Jesus the Messiah were not Jewish. Matthew's trying to tell us something. Maybe, more to the point, the Spirit is speaking.

Why Jesus? He came to show us the way to be more than just the human race. He came to show us the way to become the human family of God. Why Jesus? He came to show us how to become more than just the human race. He

---

21. The Book of Common Prayer, 281.

came to show us the way to become the human family of God. In that is our hope and salvation, now and unto the day of eternity.

That is what I suspect the Spirit is getting at through the old song:

> Join hands, disciples of the faith
> Whate'er your race may be!
> Who serves my Father as his child
> Is surely kin to me
>
> In Christ there is no East nor West
> In him no South or North
> But one great fellowship of love
> Throughout the whole wide earth.[22]

---

22. *The Hymnal 1982*, 529.

CHAPTER 3

Go Tell It on the Mountain

When I was a seeker,
I asked both night and day,
I asked the Lord to help me
And he showed me the way,

Go, tell it on the mountains,
over the hills and everywhere.
God tell it on the mountains
that Jesus Christ is born.[23]

---

23. www.songlyrics.com/fannie-lou-hammer/go-tell-it-on-the-mountain-lyrics/.

> Come, let us go to the mountain
> of the Lord, to the house of the
> God of Jacob; that he may teach
> us his ways and that we may
> walk in his paths. For out of Zion
> shall go forth instruction, and the
> word of the Lord from Jerusalem.
> He shall judge between nations,
> and shall arbitrate for many peo-
> ples; they shall beat their swords
> into plowshares, and their spears
> into pruning hooks; nation shall
> not lift up sword against nation,
> neither shall they learn war any
> more. (Isaiah 2:1–5)

The late Robert Kennedy was fond of quoting George Bernard Shaw: "Some men see things as they are and ask why. I dream things that never were and ask, why not." Isaiah of Jerusalem was someone who understood things as they were, and yet he was someone who dreamed the dream of God and asked why not. The Bible says that Isaiah began his ministry "in the year that King Uzziah died." That death, for the people of this biblical era, had much the same impact as the deaths of President Kennedy or Dr. Martin Luther King, Jr. did on those of us of a certain generation. Isaiah knew the world as it was. Much of his mature preaching occurred during the reign of King Hezekiah when the city of Jerusalem itself was under siege by the armies of Assyria. His prophecies frequently spoke of the need to end nightmares of violence and plagues of injustice.

The later sections of the book of Isaiah reflect the writings of his disciples, applying Isaiah's thought to the period of the Babylonian exile when the whole world fell apart for the people of God; when, to paraphrase Yeats, the center did not hold. Babylonian armies destroyed Jerusalem and then carted the leading citizens off like cargo to Babylon. There they lived in virtual slavery. There they languished as people without hope. There one of their poets sang these words: "By the waters of Babylon we sat down and wept when we remembered thee, O Zion. . . . How shall we sing the Lord's song in a strange land" (Psalm 137). Isaiah and his disciples spoke to such a time. Isaiah understood the world as it was.

Yet this same Isaiah was able to speak as one who dared to dream the dream of God in the midst of the nightmare that often is the world. He dreamed it and he asked, why not. Why not a world where children go to sleep fed and satisfied? Why not a world where justice rolls down like a mighty stream and righteousness like an ever-flowing brook? Why not a world where we lay down our swords and shields down by the riverside to study war no more? Why not, O Lord, why not?

Old Testament scholar Walter Brueggemann spoke of this text as "a bold and daring act of imagination."[24] Isaiah looked into the nightmare that is often the world and was able to behold the dream of God. That sanctified act of the imagination became possible because Isaiah had been to the mountain. Come, let us go to the mountain. . . .

In the Bible, the mountain is frequently a way of talking about those ways and places, those moments and memories, when God gets real, when we meet and are met by God.

Sometimes it is in those moments when we go apart to rest for a while. Sometimes it is in that "still, small voice." There is a sound in silence, if you listen. Sometimes it is when we look deeply into the face of each other to behold the *imago dei*, the image of God, the face of Jesus etched on us.

24. Walter Brueggemann, *Theology of the Old Testament: Testimony, Dispute, Advocacy* (Minneapolis: Augsburg Fortress, 1997), 501.

"When did we see you hungry, Lord?"

"When you did it to the least of these you did it to me," says Jesus.

When Dr. Martin Luther King, Jr. was murdered, he was in Memphis to stand with garbage workers who were striking for human dignity and freedom. He was looking in the face of the other when he said, "I've been to the mountaintop, and I have seen the promised land." The mountain is a way of talking about those moments when God gets real. The mountain is a way of talking about what the Celtic tradition calls those "thin places." The old song says it this way:

> Upon the mountain, my Lord spoke,
> Out of his mouth came fire and
>   smoke.
> Every time I feel the Spirit,
> Moving in my heart, I will pray.

You've got to come to the mountain! Hearts get changed on the mountain. Lives get changed on the mountain. Worlds get changed on the mountain. The mountain is the place of messianic metamorphoses.

If you do not believe me ask Abraham. Abraham went to the mountain on a mission. He thought he was engaging God's mission by sacrificing his son Isaac. But on the mountain he discovered that when it comes to God's mission, grace and mercy, compassion and faith are closer to the heart of God than either stern sacrifice or blind obedience. You've got to come to the mountain! Think about Moses. Moses went up the mountain one way, and went down another.

> Go down, Moses, way down in
>   Egypt land,
> and tell ole Pharaoh, let my people go.

You've got to come to the mountain!

In the writings of Isaiah, it is that reality on the mountain that transforms lives and can transform a world. In chapter 2, on the mountain, "they shall beat their swords into plowshares, and their spears into pruning hooks. Nation shall not rise up against nation. Neither shall they learn war anymore." In chapter 11, on the mountain, "the wolf shall lie down with the lamb." Wolves and lambs do not share the same self-interest. Dick Gregory used to say the wolf may lie down with the lamb but the lamb will not get much sleep. But on the mountain the wolf and the lamb lie down together. They dwell together. If you are like me, you have some wolf and lamb in you. On the mountain the wolf and lamb dwell together in peace: "they shall not hurt or destroy in all my holy mountain, for the earth will be filled with the glory of God as the waters cover the sea."[25] You've got to come to the mountain!

When we get to the New Testament it is no accident that there is a Sermon on the Mount. It is no accident that Jesus must go to the mountain of transfiguration before he can enter the valley of the shadow of death. It is no accident that Jesus sends the disciples on the mission to make disciples and make a difference in the world from a mountain. It is on the mountain that folk get transformed. On the mountain that enemies can become friends. On the mountain that worlds get changed. The mountain is the key to the mission. *Come, let us go to the mountain.*

I was wrestling with this passage a few years ago, and found myself stuck. I knew the mountain represented the context of Gospel transformation, but I was stuck on the question why. What was it about the mountain that can so incredibly change us all. Then I went to church. While on vacation that summer, I was visiting a church when we stood to sing Hymn 686 in

25. Isaiah 11:9.

The Hymnal 1982, "Come Thou Font of Every Blessing." I have sung that hymn all my life, but I never paid attention to the entire first verse until that day.

> Come thou font of every blessing,
> Tune my heart to sing thy grace!
>   Streams of mercy never ceasing,
> calls for songs of loudest praise.
>   Teach me some melodious sonnet,
> Sung by flaming tongues above.
>   **Praise the mount! O fix me on it, Mount of God's unchanging love.**

There it is. The mount of God's unchanging love.

The key to living the ways and teachings of God of which Isaiah speaks is living in and out of the love of God. That unchanging love can change the world. I think that is what Jesus was teaching us when he said: "You shall love the Lord your God with all your heart, soul, mind and strength. And you shall love your neighbor as yourself. On these two hang all the law and the prophets."[26] This is the Gospel. This is the

---

26. Matthew 22:40.

Good News! This is the message of the mountain and the motive of the mission. And it can change the world.

Some make the mistake of thinking of God's love as weak and anemic. Several years ago when I was blessed to be elected Bishop of North Carolina I found myself trying to explain to our then seven-year-old daughter what a bishop did. She had some sense of what I did as a parish priest, but a bishop was not quite as clear. One evening while we were eating dinner, the UPS truck pulled up to the house. The delivery guy rang the bell and my wife answered the door. It was a gift from the late Bishop Walter Dennis: a beautiful white linen miter. From that point on my daughter began to identify the miter with being a bishop. After we had moved to Raleigh she was watching a video with a friend. It was a cartoon version of the story of Dr. Martin Luther King, Jr. I happened to be walking through the den where they were watching the video. As I passed through I noticed that they were watching a scene in the story of a cross burning with hooded knights of the Ku Klux Klan. As I walked by, Elizabeth asked me, "Why are all those Episcopal bishops standing by that burning cross?"

After I told them what it was they understood, but it was not an automatic reflex.

Thirty years ago or so it would not have been possible for any black child in America not to have had a reflexive reaction of terror at that sight. Those two children, one black and one white, did not react automatically because something did change in this country and this culture. I'm here to tell you that it changed not by sword, nor by might, but by the power of God's love translated into our social situation. America is a different place because some people of all colors and kinds decided that they were going to live by love not by hatred. Love works!

Do not be afraid of it. Do not be ashamed of it. Do not underestimate the power of God's love lived out. This is the Gospel. This is the Good News. Here is our greatest strength. Here we can find healing, courage and grace. Here we find life for us and for the world. So come to the mountain. Come to the mountain of God's unchanging love. Come, there's room for us <u>all</u>. And all means <u>all</u>.

> Go, tell it on the mountain,
> over the hills and everywhere.
> Go, tell it on the mountain
> that Jesus Christ is born

CHAPTER 4

Episcopalians— Witnesses?

Send them out as witnesses to your love.
Holy Baptism, The Book of Common Prayer, page 302

So when they had come together, they asked him, "Lord, is this the time when you will restore the kingdom to Israel?" He replied, "It is not for you to know the times or periods that the Father has set by his own authority. But you will receive power when the Holy Spirit has come upon you; and you will be my witnesses in Jerusalem, in all Judea and Samaria, and to the ends of the earth." (Acts 1:5–8)

"Lord, is this the time when you will restore the kingdom to Israel?" I suspect that on some level they were asking him, "Lord, when will the many wrongs of the world be righted? When will the reign of violence, injustice, and cruelty, and hatred and bigotry come to an end? When will the rule of love and justice, and goodness and kindness be established? When will the kingdom come?"

And Jesus answered, "It is not for you to know the times or seasons that the Father has fixed by his own authority." That is a biblical way of saying, "it is not your business." There are some things you are simply not going to know. It is like that old hymn my grandma use to sing in the Baptist church, "We'll understand it better by and by." No, that is not your business.

This is your business. "You will receive power when the Holy Spirit comes upon you. And you will be my witnesses in Jerusalem, in Judea, in Samaria, and to the ends of the earth."[27] Witness—that is the business of those of us who would be disciples, followers of Jesus. We need to be witnesses!

I have been an Episcopalian my entire life. My swaddling clothes were an Episcopal flag. And this much I know: If you want to really strike terror into the heart of an Episcopalian—or, for that matter, a Presbyterian, a Lutheran, a Roman Catholic, and so on—tell them they have to go and witness. Worse, tell them they have to testify.

There is no escape. It is there in our text from Acts 1. It is there in Luke 24 where Jesus tells his disciples that it was necessary that he should die and rise from the dead and that repentance and forgiveness of sins must be proclaimed to all nations. Then he adds, "And you are witnesses of these things." In John's Gospel the word witness and testify/testimony are used over and over to describe the vocation of the servants of God. In Mark's Gospel, Jesus says that his disciples are to proclaim the Good News to the whole creation. Witness. It is all over the Bible.

I know Episcopalians, and a lot of them are lawyers. If there is a loophole, we will find

---

27. Acts of the Apostles 1:8.

it and our default loophole is the prayerbook.
If it is not in the prayerbook, we do not have
to do it. So I searched The Book of Common
Prayer, since our way of worship shapes our
hearing of Holy Scripture. On page 366 one of
the prayers after Communion says, "And now
Father, send us out to do the work you have
given us to do, to love and serve you as faithful
witnesses of Christ our Lord." No escape. On
page 855 of the Prayer Book, the Catechism,
the teaching of the church, says: "The ministry
of lay persons is to represent Christ and is
Church; to bear witness to him wherever they
may be. . . ." No escape. But maybe the most
significant commitment to the way of witness in The Book of Common Prayer is found
in Holy Baptism (and also Confirmation).
On page 302, the prayer for the candidates has
an inner movement and ascent like the old
song "We are Climbing Jacob's ladder." That
old spiritual, based on the patriarch Jacob's
dream of a ladder connecting heaven and
earth (Genesis 28), ascends from where the
singer is to the height of service to the Lord.
It begins:

  We are climbing Jacob's ladder.
  We are climbing Jacob's ladder.

We are climbing Jacob's ladder.
Soldiers of the cross.

It climbs higher:

> Every round goes higher, higher.
> Every round goes higher, higher.
> Every round goes higher, higher.
> Soldiers of the cross.

It climbs still higher:

> Sinner, do you love my Jesus?
> Sinner, do you love my Jesus?
> Sinner, do you love my Jesus?
> Soldiers of the cross.

And it finally reaches its summit:

> If you love him, why not serve him?
> If you love him, why not serve him?
> If you love him, why not serve him?
> Soldiers of the cross.

The prayer over the candidates for baptism follows a similar logic of ascent. It begins with the reality of sin and death, climbs Jacob's ladder by an amazing grace, goes through

the filling of the Holy Spirit, sustains on the
journey through the "faith and communion"
of the community of faith, grows deeper
through the teachings of love, then sends forth
as witness to the love of God, and through
this way of love reaches the last stage of the
ascent: the vision of the kingdom, the vision of
God:

> Deliver them, O Lord, from the way
>   of sin and death.
> Open their hearts to your grace and
>   truth.
> Fill them with your holy and
>   life-giving Spirit.
> Keep them in the faith and
>   communion of your holy Church.
> Teach them to love others in the
>   power of the Spirit.
> Send them into the world in witness
>   to your love.
> Bring them to the fullness of your
>   peace and glory.

If we are going to follow Jesus, we have to witness. Now I know what the problem is. When
we hear the word "witness" most of us, myself

included, probably think of Saturday morning. We are at home minding our own business, having a cup of coffee, when the doorbell rings. At the door are two nicely dressed people with little bags and copies of *Watchtower* magazine. And we want to hide. Witness? Or, perhaps we remember that time somebody came up and out of the blue asked, "Are you saved?" or "Have you been born again?" or "Will you be left behind?" Witness? I get it. Maybe the Bible can help us here. In the Sermon on the Mount (Matthew 5—7) Matthew has brought together some of Jesus's core teachings on what being a disciple of his looks like. At one point he says:

> You are the light of the world. A city built on a hill cannot be hid. No one after lighting a lamp puts it under the bushel basket, but on the lampstand, and it gives light to all in the house. In the same way, let your light shine before others, so that they may see your good works and give glory to your Father in heaven. (Matthew 5:14–16)

He was talking about witness. You know the song based on this text.

> This little light of mine, I'm gonna
> let it shine,
> This little light of mine, I'm gonna
> let it shine,
> This little light of mine, I'm gonna
> let it shine,
> Let it shine, let it shine, let it shine.

Witness. And one of the stanzas continues.

> Everywhere I go, I'm gonna let it
> shine,
> Everywhere I go, I'm gonna let it
> shine,
> Everywhere I go, I'm gonna let it
> shine,
> Let it shine, let it shine, let it shine.

Jesus was talking about witness.

Just before Jesus named his followers the light of the world, he taught them what following him looks like. He said,

Blessed are the poor and the poor in spirit.

Blessed are the merciful, the compassionate.

Blessed are those who hunger and thirst that God's righteous justice might prevail in the world.

Blessed are the peacemakers.

Blessed are you when you are persecuted just because you tried to love somebody. Rejoice and be exceedingly glad for so they persecuted the prophets who were before you.

Love your enemies. Blessed those who curse you. Pray for those who despitefully use you. When you live like that, you will look like me.

And you will be the salt of the earth!

You will help to bring out the flavor that God intended from the beginning.

You will be the light of the world!

Your life will illuminate what God intended the world to look like in the beginning.

And in so doing you will change the world. For you will be my light in the world.

And you will witness

> This little light of mine, I'm gonna
>   let it shine,
> This little light of mine, I'm gonna
>   let it shine,

This little light of mine, I'm gonna
  let it shine,
Let it shine, let it shine, let it shine.

We need some witnesses like that.

CHAPTER 5

Jesus's Family Values

"Truly I tell you, many will come
from east and west and will eat with
Abraham and Isaac and Jacob in the
kingdom of heaven." (Matthew 8:11)

In Christ there is no East or West
In him no South or North
But one great fellowship of love
Throughout the whole wide earth.

Jesus came to show us the way to become more
than we ever could, or would, be on our own.

Another way to say it is God came among us in the person of Jesus of Nazareth to show us the way to be right and reconciled with the God who created us all, and with each other as children of that one God and Father of us all.

Consider this healing story. It is not an ordinary healing. It is about healing a lot more than the body. Let me show you what I mean.

> When he entered Capernaum, a centurion came to him, appealing to him and saying, "Lord, my servant is lying at home paralyzed, in terrible distress." And he said to him, "I will come and cure him." The centurion answered, "Lord, I am not worthy to have you come under my roof; but only speak the word, and my servant will be healed. For I also am a man under authority, with soldiers under me; and I say to one, 'Go,' and he goes, and to another, 'Come,' and he comes, and to my slave, 'Do this,' and the slave does it." When Jesus heard him, he was amazed and said to those who followed him, "Truly I tell you, in no one in Israel have I found such faith. I tell you, many

> will come from east and west
> and will eat with Abraham and
> Isaac and Jacob in the kingdom of
> heaven. (Matthew 8:5–11)

Matthew's telling of the healing of the slave of a Roman centurion is nothing short of extraordinary. Just think about the sociology of the story. Remember the Jewish people were a colonized people. They had long ago lost their freedom. Against their will and desire they were a colonial outpost of the Empire of Rome. They were an occupied country. Roman soldiers ruled the land. And the rulers of Rome were not in the spirit of Plato's philosopher kings. They were dictators, tyrants with the Imperial army of Rome as the muscle behind it all.

That makes the interaction between the Roman centurion—a master sergeant in the Roman army—all the more extraordinary. Think about it: here you have a leader of the occupying forces, the kind of soldier who often made Jews carry their bags for miles, the kind of soldier who was likely a pagan adherent of the religious traditions of Greece and Rome, beseeching, imploring, begging Jesus, an itinerate, Palestinian Jewish rabbi to heal his own servant. No, 'servant' is too polite. He was the slave of the centurion. He was likely someone who had been defeated and captured in battle. He was a man whose freedom had been taken away by the same Roman soldier who was now begging for his healing.

This is simply extraordinary. Every conceivable line of division is being crossed here. They are from different religions, different ethnicities, different political ideologies, different social classes. They are enemies. Oppressor and oppressed. Here the oppressor begs the oppressed on behalf of another member of an oppressed class.

> My servant is sick, I need you to heal him. Please, I beg you. I'm not worthy to have you come to my house. If you just speak the word. Command the host of heaven.
>
> I know, I'm a soldier, I know what it is to give orders and commands, and I give an order and it is executed. But I know you can command the illness to depart and it will obey you. There is something about God in you. I just know it. Please. I beg you, Jesus. Please!

And Jesus was blown away by this and moved deeply. And then he says something remarkable.

> When Jesus heard him, he was
> amazed and said to those who
> followed him, 'Truly I tell you,
> in no one in Israel have I found
> such faith. I tell you, many will
> come from east and west and will
> eat with Abraham and Isaac and
> Jacob in the kingdom of heaven.

Did Matthew tell the story this way because
in it he saw God's promise of blessing through
Abraham being fulfilled through Jesus, son of
Abraham? Did Matthew sense that through
this Jesus God was creating a new human
family, born not of blood, but out of love? I
can't prove it but it sure makes sense to me.

> Join hands disciples of the faith
> What-e're your race may be
> Who serves my Father as his child
> Is surely kin to me
>
> In Christ there is no East or West
> In him no South or North
> But one great fellowship of love
> Throughout the whole wide earth.

God came among us in the Person of Jesus to
show us the way to become more than merely

the human race. That is not good enough. We can do better than that. Jesus came to show us the way to become the human family of God and in that is our hope and our eternal salvation. Nowhere is that more pointedly demonstrated than in Jesus's creation of the parable of the Last Judgment.

> When the Son of Man comes in his glory, and all the angels with him, then he will sit on the throne of his glory. All the nations will be gathered before him, and he will separate people one from another as a shepherd separates the sheep from the goats, and he will put the sheep at his right hand and the goats at the left. Then the king will say to those at his right hand, "Come, you that are blessed by my Father, inherit the kingdom prepared for you from the foundation of the world; for I was hungry and you gave me food, I was thirsty and you gave me something to drink, I was a stranger and you welcomed me, I was naked and you gave me clothing, I was sick and you took

care of me, I was in prison and you
visited me." (Matthew 25:31–36)

Professor Bill Brosend of the School of Theology
at the University of the South recently came
to spend time with the clergy here in North
Carolina, working on our preaching. In one of
his talks he spoke about the spiritual genius
of the parables of Jesus. In them, he told us,
we are actually getting something very close
to the mind of the Master, the very heart of
God because the parables are made-up stories.
Jesus made them up to point to deeper truths
about life and eternity than laws or commentary without spirit can ever suggest. It is mind
blowing to think that in these creative stories
of Jesus, called parables, we are looking deeply
into his creative, loving, liberating heart and
mind. When Bill said that I was blown away.
He was right. In these made-up stories intended
to draw us into the deep things of God and life
and death, hurt, and hope and healing, we are
looking into the heart and mind of God.

The parable of the Last Judgment in Matthew
25 is one of those extraordinary stories of Jesus
that looks into the heart of God: what matters
to God. Jesus says that at the conclusion and
completion of all time and history, on judgment

day, at that "great gett'n up morning," as the slaves used to say, the Lord will descend from the realm of heaven in all of his glory. Before him will be arrayed all the nations of the earth—all stripes and types of people—and the Lord will administer justice. To the righteous, the just ones of the earth, he says:

> Then the king will say to those at his right hand, "Come, you that are blessed by my Father, inherit the kingdom prepared for you from the foundation of the world; for I was hungry and you gave me food, I was thirsty and you gave me something to drink, I was a stranger and you welcomed me, I was naked and you gave me clothing, I was sick and you took care of me, I was in prison and you visited me." (Matthew 25:34–37)

I can imagine the righteous ones thinking, *Lord, we are glad we're going to heaven, but when did we see you hungry and feed you or naked and cloth you, or alone and visit you. Don't misunderstand. We are very grateful. We want to go to heaven. But for the life of us, we do not remember seeing you need us.* That is when Jesus says: "Truly I tell you, just as you did it to one of the least of these who are members of my family, you did it to me."

When I went off to college my father gave me the father-son lecture one last time. He tried to be subtle about it but I knew exactly what he was doing. Now that I'm the father of two daughters and a grandfather, I really know exactly what he was doing. He said a number of things but I remember one thing in particular that has stayed with me these many years. He said, "Remember to treat every girl the way you want somebody else to treat your sister."

There was a part of me that was thinking, "You just ruined four years of college," but he was right. He was saying something pretty significant: relate to every girl and woman as if they were your sister, because they are. Relate to every boy and man like you would your brother, because they are. The love you have for your own flesh and blood is the love you are to have for every man, woman, and child because we are all children of the one God and Father who created us all. That is what is behind the incredible claims Jesus and the New Testament make about love. Professor Dierdre Goode calls these *Jesus's family* values.

Consider what he taught us. *Love your enemies. Bless those who curse you. Pray for those who
despitefully use you.* Why? <u>They are your family!</u>
These are Jesus's family values. *As the Father has
loved me, so have I loved you. Abide in my love. A
new commandment I give you, that you love one
another.* Why? <u>They are your family!</u> *By this
everyone will know that you are my disciples, that
you love one another.* Why? You are <u>family!</u> *Though
I speak with the tongues of men and of angels, and
have not love, I am a noisy gong, a clanging cym-
bala. Now faith, hope, love abide, these three, but the
greatest of these is love.* <u>You are family!</u>

Here is the foundation of it all. *You shall love
the Lord your God with all your heart, all your
soul, all your mind, and all your strength. This is
the first and great commandment. And the second
is like it. You shall love your neighbor as yourself.
On these two hang all the law and the prophets.*

God came among us in the person of Jesus
to show us the way to be right and reconciled
with the God who created us all, and the way to
be right and reconciled with each other as God's
children. In so doing he came to show us the way
to become more than the human race. He came
to show us the way to become the human family
of God. That is what his kingship, that is what
his Lordship, that is what his kingdom, his rule,

his reign, his dominion is about. Jesus's family values are about becoming the human family of God, reconciled with God and each other. And in that way is hope and salvation for us all.

In both a documentary film called *God's House*, and a photographic essay titled *Besa: Muslims Who Saved Jews during World War II*, photographer Norman Gershman tells a little-known story of the Muslims of Albania from the Second World War. Europe was being conquered by armies of the Third Reich. Jews were being rounded up throughout Europe for imprisonment and death. As the Nazis approached Albania, Medi Frasheri, the Albanian Prime Minister, who was a Muslim, refused to release the names of Jews who were living in Albania. He organized an underground movement from the Muslim community.

Haxhi Dede Reshat Bardhi, who was interviewed by Gershman for the book, recalls the Prime Minister's orders to the Muslim community of Albania at the time: "All Jewish children will sleep with your children, all will eat the same food, all will live as one family."[28] As he told this to Gershman in the interview, he

28. Norman H. Gershman, *Besa: Muslims Who Saved Jews In World War II* (Syracuse, NY: Syracuse University Press, 2008), 4.

went on to explain where this extraordinary perspective came from.

> We Bektashi see God everywhere,
> in everyone. God is in every pore
> and every cell, therefore all are
> God's children. There cannot be
> infidels. There cannot be discrim-
> ination. If one sees a good face
> one is seeing the face of God.[29]

As a result of this deep conviction and the quiet courage it created, this small community of Muslims saved over two thousand Jews from the death camps. This looks like Jesus's family values to me. He came to show us the way to become more than merely a collection of individual, ethnic, national, ideological, or even religious self-interests. God came among us in the person of Jesus of Nazareth to show us the way to overcome our nightmare and realize God's dream.

> "I have a dream," God says.
> "Please help Me to realize it. It is
> a dream of a world whose ugliness

29. *Ibid.*

and squalor and poverty, its war and hostility, its greed and harsh competitiveness, its alienation and disharmony are changed into their glorious counterparts, when there will be more laughter, joy, and peace, where there will be justice and goodness and compassion and love and caring and sharing. I have a dream that swords will be beaten into plowshares and spears into pruning hooks, that My children will know that they are members of one family, the human family, God's family, My family."

In God's family, there are no outsiders. All are insiders. Black and white, rich and poor, gay and straight, Jew and Arab, Palestinian and Israeli, Roman Catholic and Protestant, Serb and Albanian, Hutu and Tutsi, Muslim and Christian, Buddhist and Hindu, Pakistani and Indian—all belong.[30]

---

30. Desmond Tutu, *God Has a Dream: A Vision of Hope for Our Time* (New York: Image Book, Doubleday, 2005).

Our vocation as disciples of Jesus is to live out his family values in personal living and public witness, to help God realize God's dream.

> Join hands disciples of the faith
> Whate'er your race may be
> Who serves my Father as his child
> Is surely kin to me
>
> In Christ there is no East or West
> In him no South or North
> But one great fellowship of love
> Throughout the whole wide earth.

CHAPTER 6

Glory!

There are some words so old, time tested, and venerable that they are capable of bearing within them enormous freight and weight of insight for the living of these days. Such words have been around long enough to point with some accuracy, based on experience, to those sacred moments when Diving Providence and human personality work together, and human life and sometimes history are changed. One such word is the biblical word, "Glory."

"Glory" is the title and recurring theme in John Legend and Common's stunning song that concludes *Selma*, a film that retells the story of the Civil Rights struggle for human equality and the right to vote for all Americans. The song brilliantly combines the soulful heart of Gospel music, the poetic cadences of hip hop, and the deep, sometimes mournful wisdom of the spirituals once sung by slaves. Glory!

In the Bible the glory of the Lord is realized when the world, when life, when the creation is reconfigured from the nightmare we often make into the dream that God has intended since God first declared, "Let there be light." When evil is overcome by good, therein is the glory of the Lord. When ancient wrongs are put to flight and right overcomes might, therein is God's glory. When love becomes the root of law and justice conquers injustice, therein is glory.

And at the end of *Selma*, after so many had sacrificed, suffered, struggled, and died, when the good did in the end overcome, and the 1965 Voting Rights Bill became law, the song "Glory" provides a metaphor for the moment when the Providence of God in partnership with ordinary people changed the course of history like the parting of the Red Sea. Glory!

Glory! It's a word you would hear when you went to grandma's church when the preacher preached and the word became flesh and folk felt it, and everybody knew it. Glory!

It's an old word saturated with the Spirit of the Ancient of Days. Glory!

In a stunning poetic vision, the prophet Isaiah envisions the world reconfigured from the nightmare it often is into the dream that God intends. He sees great mountains of conceit and arrogant power brought low. He sees valleys of the humiliated and dispossessed raised up. He sees crooked ways of injustice straightened out into God's way of justice, and the rough ways made easy by the smooth way of love. In it all the prophet sees the revelation of the glory of God.

> A voice cries out:
> "In the wilderness prepare the way of the Lord, make straight in the desert a highway for our God. Every valley shall be lifted up, and every mountain and hill be made low; the uneven ground shall become level, and the rough places a plain. Then the glory of the Lord shall be revealed, and all people shall see it together, for the

mouth of the Lord has spoken.
(Isaiah 40:3–5)

Capturing the true essence of the spiritual struggle behind the Civil War, Julia Ward Howe called on that word:

> In the beauty of the lilies, Christ
>   was born across the sea,
> With a glory in his bosom, that
>   transfigured you and me:
> As he died to make men holy, let us
>   die to make men free,
> While God is marching on.
>
> Glory, glory hallelujah,
> Glory, glory hallelujah,
> Glory, glory hallelujah,
> God's truth is marching on.[31]

My old friend Charles Marsh recently published a book on the life of Dietrich Bonhoeffer, the result of years of study of his life, thought, and witness. Charles titled his book, *Strange Glory*. The title was taken from a sermon of Bonhoeffer's, a man whose witness to Jesus included the sacrifice of his own life in his

---

31. "Mine Eyes Have Seen the Glory," Julia Ward Howe (1819–1910).

stand against Nazism and for the love of God revealed in the way of Jesus. It is the full sentence from Bonhoeffer's sermon, however, that makes the point more directly: "It is a strange glory, the glory of this God."[32] John's Gospel called on that word to give voice to the inner meaning of the sacrifice of Jesus for the cause of the God "who so loved the world that he gave his only son."

> After Jesus had spoken these words, he looked up to heaven and said, "Father, the hour has come; glorify your Son so that the Son may glorify you, since you have given him authority over all people, to give eternal life to all whom you have given him. And this is eternal life, that they may know you, the only true God and Jesus Christ whom you have sent. I glorified you on earth by finishing the work that you gave me to do. So now, Father, glorify me in your own presence with the glory that I had in your presence before the world existed." (John 17:1–5)

---

32. Dietrich Bonhoeffer, London Sermon, 1933.

Glory!

The late professor Raymond Brown in his magisterial commentary on the Gospel of John offers a perceptive analysis of the use of the word "glory" in John's gospel. He says if you look carefully you will notice the book divides neatly into two sections. Chapters 1–11 function as part one of the Gospel. He calls this section, "The Book of Signs." Chapters 12–21 are part two, which he calls "The Book of Glory."

In part one the focus of the Gospel is on the miracles of Jesus which John's Gospel calls signs. When Jesus turns water into wine, John says, this was "the first of his signs" (John 2:11). He heals the crippled man. He feeds the multitude. He walks on water. He restores the sight of the blind man. He raises old Lazarus from the dead with the thunderous words, "Lazarus, come forth." And after each of these miracles the Gospel says, this was the first sign, the second sign, and on and on. Professor Brown is correct in calling part one of John's Gospel, "The Book of Signs."

The second part of the gospel Brown calls "The Book of Glory" because beginning with the twelfth chapter Jesus no longer performs miracles but begins to talk about glory. "Now my soul is troubled. Father, glorify your name" (John 12:27). Over and over he speaks of glory from chapters twelve through seventeen. GLORY. 'Tis a strange thing, this glory. The paradox of this shift in vocabulary is that it happens during the recounting of the passion and crucifixion of Jesus. It is in the shadow of the cross that the Master begins to speak of glory. As he washes the feet of his disciples—Glory! As Judas slithers out of the room—Glory! As the cock crows the second time and a fateful word is spoken, "I do not know him"—Glory! As sacred blood stains an old rugged cross—Glory!

Some time ago the *Parade* magazine supplement of our Sunday paper featured a cover story on the Olympic games. The title of the story was "Going for Glory."[33] That is what I know as glory. Glory is when you win the race. Glory is when success is yours. Glory is when I have got a crown on my head, not a cross on my shoulders. Glory is when the crowd cheers, not when they shout "let him be crucified." Glory is when you have graduated, when you have gotten married, when you have had a baby, when your teenager leaves home. That is glory. Glory is when you're on the mountaintop, not in "the valley of the shadow of death." It is therefore rather strange, ironic,

---

33. *Parade*, Sunday, September 10, 2000.

and paradoxical that Jesus only speaks of glory as he nears the shadow of the cross.

The key to making sense of this is in the text itself. Listen to Jesus again, at the Last Supper (John 17:4): "[Father,] I glorify you on earth by finishing the work that you gave me to do." Jesus discovered the glory of God as he fulfilled his destiny by being who he was in the first place. *I glorify you on earth by finishing the work that you gave me to do.*

The movie *Chariots of Fire* retells the story of the 1924 Summer Olympics in Paris. A runner named Eric Liddel from Scotland ran for Great Britain. He was fast. He was the Michael Johnson of his day. You may remember Michael Johnson from the Atlanta Olympics. He ran so fast that he left everyone else in the dust. Eric Liddel was like him. He was quick. He was able. He ran effortlessly. It almost seemed as though he did not even sweat.

Liddel had gained a great deal of notoriety before the Olympics and everyone was looking forward to his running in the great race. He came from a great Scottish Presbyterian missionary family. They believed it was important for him to be involved in the mission field. His sister asked him if he would forgo running in the Olympics and join the family in China in missionary work. It was a difficult moment for him. He loved to run. He loved to be a missionary and he was torn between the two. Finally, after some soul-searching and great thought, Liddel came back to his sister and he told her that it was not time for him to go to China yet. He explained it by saying: "God made me fast and when I run I feel his pleasure." That is glory!

The early Church thinker Irenaeus of Lyons once taught that "the glory of God is humanity fully alive." "God made me fast and when I run I feel his pleasure." Glory!

God made me, me and God made you, YOU. And when you are YOU, when you run the race that is set before YOU, you feel his pleasure. Glory. We glorify God by being the persons God created us to be. Our power is there. Our strength is there. Our beauty is there. YOU are incredibly beautiful. God is glorified as you become the you that God has dreamed and intended from the moment of your creation. Jesus taught us that.

You will remember these words. They are sometimes quoted as an Offertory Sentence before taking up the collection. They come from the Sermon on the Mount (Matthew 5:16). "Let your light so shine before others so that they may see your good works and give glory to your Father in Heaven." Notice that it is as you let your light shine that you glorify God. When I let my light shine, I glorify God. I cannot shine for you. You cannot shine for me. But I have to shine for me and when I truly shine, the real me, the me created in the image and likeness of God, the me not controlled, marred or scarred by the ravages of self-centered sinfulness, when I shine, when I'm the real Michael, then God is glorified.

Another old spiritual sings it this way:

> Glory, glory, hallelujah.
> Since I laid my burdens down.
>
> I feel better,
> so much better.
> Since I laid my burden down.
>
> Glory, glory, hallelujah.
> Since I laid my burdens down.

Harry Emerson Fosdick, arguably one of the greatest Gospel preachers of the twentieth century, composed a poem that has become one of the great hymns of the church. The context of the composition is worth noting. It was the war years of World War II. A country still reeling from vast poverty and economic suffering of the Great Depression was now reeling from war against the dark clouds of totalitarian fascism, racism, and imperialism. People survived the Depression only to receive telegrams informing them of the death of a son, a grandson, a child in battle. It was a difficult, horrible, and painful time. It was in his crucible of hard times that Fosdick wrote of this strange glory as hope.

> God of grace and God of glory
> On thy people pour thy power
> Crown thy church's ancient story
> Bring her bud to glorious flower
> Grant us wisdom, grant us courage
> For the facing of this hour

Let God truly be glorified

By a world in which children do not go to bed hungry

By a world in which the creation is reverenced and cared for;

By a world in which love is the law by which we live

And where we have learned to lay down our swords and shields down by the riverside to study war no more.

> "One day, when the glory comes
> It will be ours, it will be ours."

Thanks be to God.

CHAPTER 7

A Song Seldom Sung

For many years, Cecil B. DeMille's film *The Ten Commandments* was shown on television either on Palm Sunday or Easter. My grandmother, like other folk in her world, would watch as faithfully as she watched Gomer Pyle, Bonanza, Billy Graham—and Martin Luther King, Jr., any time he appeared on the screen. My sister and I would often watch with her, even into our teenage years. Invariably, at some point during the film's telling of the biblical story of the freedom struggle of Hebrew slaves long ago she would say at least once, "God moves in mysterious ways." She said it on other occasions, too. Where that came from for her I never asked. Though it was a hymn, I never heard her or anyone else in the world I grew up in actually sing it, but the words were recited often as a kind of creed-like affirmation.

When I was a young priest serving in my first congregation in Winston Salem, North Carolina, I selected the hymn to be sung one Sunday. It had been suggested in a guidebook for pairing hymns with the readings assigned in the lectionary for any given Sunday. The words clearly fit the biblical texts for the day, but I never scheduled the hymn again. No one knew the tune, though everyone seemed to know the words of the first stanza.

Say the words, "What a friend we have in Jesus," and a tune comes to mind for generations of folks raised by or near my grandmother's world. Say the words, "Just as I am, without one plea," and a song starts singing in my conscious-ness. Say the words, "Amazing grace, how sweet the sound that saved a wretch like me," and music comes to mind. But say, "God moves in mysterious ways," and no melody makes its way into my mind. I am aware that in other places in the English-speaking world the hymn has some resonance, but not so much in the southern U.S. even though the opening phrase was once recited like an old familiar song.

Like many hymns, it had its origin in a poem that captured the Christian imagination for many. It was written by William Cowper (1731–1800), the author of several poems that are now hymn texts. He was a person of deep and complex faith, an English evangelical associated with John Newton ("Amazing Grace") and others involved in both the evangelical movement and the movement to bring an end to the slave trade. In a time with limited therapeutic and medical treatment he, like so many, struggled mightily with depression. Just knowing that adds some depth to what otherwise could be misread as piety born of superficial spirituality. Invoking the lofty poetry that John's gospel uses to introduce Jesus, "The light shines in the darkness, and the darkness did not overcome it," Cowper titled the poem, "Light Shining Out Of Darkness."

> God moves in a mysterious way
> His wonders to perform;
> He plants his footsteps in the sea,
> And rides upon the storm.

Deep in unfathomable mines,
With never-failing skill,
He treasures up his bright designs
And works his sovereign will.

Ye fearful saints, fresh courage take;
The clouds ye so much dread
Are big with mercy, and shall break
In blessings on your head.

Judge not the Lord by feeble sense,
But trust him for his grace;
Behind a frowning providence
He hides a smiling face.

His purposes will ripen fast,
Unfolding every hour;
The bud may have a bitter taste,
But sweet will be the flower.

Blind unbelief is sure to err
And scan His work in vain;
God is his own interpreter,
And he will make it plain.[34]

How the words of that hymn/poem entered the
spiritual consciousness of my grandmother and
her generation I do not know, but they did. Even

---

34. *The Hymnal 1982*, 677.

though it was not sung with the lips, it was lived, and formed a sort of libretto of life. Sometimes the first lines were spoken in moments of deep perplexity, profound personal puzzlement, and in hard times when, as James Weldon Johnson once said, "hope unborn had died."

God moves in a mysterious way . . .

But then, the second part was often added when hope had been successfully wrestled from the clutches of hopelessness, when the good, the just, the loving could, by a faith born not of this world, be trusted to engage the seeming titanic power of hatred, of bigotry, of evil, of sin, of wrong, injustice, wickedness.

For my grandmother's generation of African Americans deeply rooted in Jim Crow's land in the years that included the War to End All Wars, the Great Depression, and World War II, the complete text was spoken when Booker T. Washington was invited to the White House by Theodore Roosevelt or when Jesse Owens defeated Adolf Hitler's master race in the Olympics. *God moves in mysterious ways his wonders to perform.* They sang it when the Tuskegee Airmen went into battle and won. They sang it when Franklin Roosevelt issued Executive

Order 8802 integrating the defense industries. They sang when Harry Truman desegregated the military. They sang when the Supreme Court spoke in Brown vs Board of Education of Topeka, Kansas. God moves in mysterious ways, his wonders to perform. When goodness was overcoming wickedness, when right was showing its might, when Caesar's law was being interpreted or changed to reflect the love of Christ, when justice was on the verge of or actually being done and a victory nearly won, they sang.

> God moves in a mysterious way
> His wonders to perform;
> He plants his footsteps in the sea
> And rides upon the storm.

But this was not, as the life of the poet suggests, born of a saccharine-sweet spirituality. That hymn and the poem that birthed it bear much wisdom about the real God and about life as it is really lived. There is no pretense that storms do not come, that hard times aren't for real, that life can be painful, sorrowful, horrible, and even awful. No grinning God. No fairy tale faith. But a real and durable faith that can wrestle with life, like Jacob wrestling with the angel, claiming a victory even

when you walk with a limp as a result of the
struggle.

> Ye fearful saints, fresh courage take;
> The clouds ye so much dread
> Are big with mercy and shall break
> In blessings on your head.
> Judge not the Lord by feeble sense,
> But trust Him for His grace;
> Behind a frowning providence
> He hides a smiling face.

Dig down deep into the meaning of the meta-
phors and there is wisdom for living. The
words of that hymn remind me of something
theologian Paul Tillich said in a sermon.

> Providence does not mean a divine
> planning by which everything is
> predetermined, as is in an effi-
> cient machine. Rather, Providence
> means that there is a creative
> and saving possibility implied in
> every situation which cannot be
> destroyed by any event.[35]

---

35. Paul Tillich, "The Meaning of Providence," *The Shaking of the
Foundations* (New York: C. Scribner and Sons, 1948).

The Providence of God, which is what the hymn is singing about, does not mean that bad things do not happen to good people, or that bad things do not happen. They do. Accidents happen. Folk get sick. Injustices occur. Everyone dies. The Providence of God means that with God there is always, even in the bleakest of circumstances, another possibility. A creative, a hopeful, a life giving possibility. That is why prayer matters—not because it is like rubbing a rabbit's foot or making a wish to get what we want, but because prayer is about daring to consider the creative possibilities of God, and not just the limits of our options.

That is why faith is not an escape from life but a way of deeper engagement to discover creative possibilities.

That is why miracles are not the magical manipulation of the cosmos but the unveiling of creative possibilities not noticed or previously envisioned.

That is why hope endures. It never gives up. For with God there is always another possibility.

And that is why, in the end, love wins. For,

> Behind a frowning providence
> He hides a smiling face.

To borrow from the late Howard Thurman, at the heart of it all, there is a heart. And if that is true, then life can be lived, no matter what, with courage, power, and love. In a meditation on words of the spiritual, "Wade in the water, God's gonna trouble the water," Thurman says this quite powerfully:

> Here we are face to face with perhaps the most daring and revolutionary concept known to man: namely, that God is not only the creative mind and spirit at the core of the universe but that He—and mark you, I say He—is love. . . . There is at the heart of life a Heart. When such an insight is possessed by the human spirit and possesses the human spirit, a vast and awe-inspiring tranquility irradiates the life. This is the message of the spiritual. Do not shrink from moving confidently out into choppy seas. Wade in the water, because God is troubling the water.[36]

---

36. Howard Thurman, *Deep River and the Negro Spiritual Speaks of Life and Death* (Richmond, IN: Friends United Press, 1975), 94.

Life grounded in such a faith can be lived with courage. As Paul said it, "With God before us who can be against us." Or as Bishop Barbara Harris often says, "The God behind you is greater than any problem ahead of you."

I saw that in this woman who happened to be my grandmother. Don't misunderstand me. I do not wish to make her more in death than she could have been in life. Like us all she was that curious mixture of saint and sinner. But I saw in her what Paul Tillich called "the courage to be": the courage to live life with dignity, integrity, vitality, life saturated by eternity, in spite of sin, injustice, and even death.

Nellie Strayhorne was born to generations who remembered what slavery was, not for the Hebrews in Egypt, but for them in antebellum America; not merely as ancient history, but recent memory. She was raised in the midst of the new economic slavery of sharecropping and the nightmare of hooded nightriders setting fire to crosses burning in the night. She did domestic work herself but saw her children through college. She buried a husband and one of her children along the way.

Though she surely had her ups and downs, I never saw her live as if defeated. There was a sense of nobility and courage in the face of both life and death. That was "the courage to be," born by living into God's new possibility and not simply human reality. If the God "behind you is greater than any problem ahead of you," there is always another possibility, a creative, saving, liberating, life giving possibility, and if that is true you can "keep hope alive."

This may be one of the great insights of the Bible. It emerges at crucial moments in the Hebrew-Christian saga of Scripture. It is there in creation, in the exodus, in the incarnation, and in the resurrection. With God there is always another possibility. You can see it in the poetry of creation in Genesis:

> In the beginning when God created the heavens and the earth, the earth was a formless void and darkness covered the face of the deep, while a wind from God swept over the face of the waters. Then God said, "Let there be light"; and there was light. (Genesis 1:1–3)

The Hebrew poet's language describing "a formless void" and "darkness [covering] the face of the deep" is a poetic way of talking about the chaos of nothingness. For before God called creation into being there was chaos, not creation, nothing, not something. Yet with God there is always another possibility and "in the beginning," that other possibility was creation, being, life, the world, us. "And God said, let there be. . . .and there was."

You can see it, as we suggested earlier, in the story of the Exodus. The escaping Hebrew slaves were trapped: Red Sea before them and the Egyptian army behind them. There was no exit, no way out, no hope. Yet with God there is always another possibility and God parted the Red Sea and set the captives free.

You can see it in the birth stories about Jesus. Mary, described as a virgin, is pregnant. She is engaged. She has been faithful. "How can this be," she asks. And the reply she receives from the messenger of God is this: "For nothing will be impossible with God" (Luke 1:26–38). With God there is always another possibility.

You can see it in the resurrection of Jesus from the dead. Even Mary Magdalene and some of the other women disciples who went to the tomb that Sunday morning didn't go expecting to find Jesus alive. They went to do what loved ones do. They went to keep faith. They went to keep vigil. They went to perform the liturgies of love for a loved one now dead. They did not go expecting Jesus to be alive. Dead folk do not come back to life in the first century or the twenty-first, except in horror movies. (And in the movies, when they do, it is not a particularly happy thing.) More to the point, a large stone had been placed before the tomb, eclipsing all hope. They had no way of moving the stone.

When the women arrived at the tomb, the stone had been rolled away. One version of the story says there was an earthquake. Another speaks of angels. The point is that with God there is always another possibility. Death does not have the final word. Neither does evil. Neither does injustice. Neither does sin. Neither does hurt, harm or hell. God is the alpha and the omega, the beginning and the end. With God there is another possibility.

> But the angel said to the women, "Do not be afraid; I know that you are looking for Jesus who was crucified. He is not here; for he has been raised, as he said." (Matthew 28:5–6)

> *God moves in a mysterious way,*
> *HIs wonders to perform.*

With God there is always another possibility. And even at the end, the Bible reaches toward its crescendo with this declaration.

> Then I saw a new heaven and a new earth; for the first heaven and the first earth had passed away, and the sea was no more. And I saw the holy city, the new Jerusalem, coming down out of heaven from God, prepared as a bride adorned for her husband.
> And I heard a loud voice from the throne saying,

> "See, the home of God is among
>   mortals.
> He will dwell with them;
> they will be his peoples,
> and God himself will be with them;
> he will wipe every tear from their
>   eyes.
> Death will be no more;
> mourning and crying and pain will
>   be no more,
> for the first things have passed
>   away."

And the one who was seated on
the throne said, "See, I am making
all things new."
(Revelation 21:1–5)

Signs for the "adopt a highway" program can
be seen along many roads throughout the
country. Usually clubs, fraternities, sororities,
or other community groups adopt a section of
a public highway. They pick up litter and gene-
rally help to keep it fresh and nice looking.
For that, the group is named somewhere along
the road. This program has turned out to be a
great help. I do not know for sure, but I suspect
this is one of the carry overs from the "Keep
America Beautiful" campaign of the 1960s. As
with anything good someone always comes
along to mess things up. As was the case in
the biblical Eden, there is always a snake in
the garden. Some time ago the Ku Klux Klan
in Missouri requested the right to participate
in the adopt-a-highway program. State officials
declined the request, but the Klan took them
to court. Regretfully the court ordered the
state to give the Klan a section of the highway
to take care of. They obeyed the order. The

state legislature then renamed the highway,
the Rosa Parks Highway.

> God moves in a mysterious way
> His wonders to perform;
> He plants his footsteps in the sea
> And rides upon the storm.

CHAPTER 8

Ride On!

Ride on King Jesus!
No man can hinder me
Ride on King Jesus!
No man can hinder me

"Rejoice greatly, O daughter of
  Zion!
Shout aloud, O daughter of
  Jerusalem!
Lo, your king comes to you;
  triumphant and victorious is he,

humble and riding on a donkey, on
a colt, the foal of a donkey."
(Zechariah 9:9)

Malala Yousafzai was shot and nearly killed
by the Taliban in Pakistan because of her
advocacy for the right of girls and all children
to education. She was fifteen years old at the
time. In 2014, at the age of seventeen, she was
awarded the Nobel Peace Prize. In both her
book *I am Malala* and her Nobel lecture she
summoned forth the depth of her faith as the
ground on which she stood for the cause of
the good.

> I love my God. I thank my Allah.
> I talk to him all day. He is the
> greatest. By giving me this height
> to reach people, he has also given
> me great responsibilities. Peace in
> every home, every street, every
> village, every country – this is my
> dream. Education for every boy
> and every girl in the world.[37]

37. Malala Yousafzai, *I Am Malala* (New York: Little, Brown and Company 2013), 313.

Ride on King Jesus!
No man can hinder me
Ride on King Jesus!
No man can hinder me

Aung San Suu Kyi, who was awarded the Nobel Prize in 1991 for her leadership in the nonviolent struggle for democracy and human rights in Myanmar, echoed the same kind of conviction summoning up deep wisdom from her Buddhist tradition. In his presentation speech when she was awarded the Prize, the Chair of the Nobel Committee quoted her words:

> The Burmese associate peace and
> security with coolness and shade:
> "The shade of a tree is cool indeed
> The shade of parents is cooler
> The shade of teachers is cooler still
> The shade of the ruler is yet more
>   cool
> But coolest of all is the shade of the
>   Buddha's teachings."
> Thus to provide the people with
> the protective coolness of peace
> and security, rulers must observe
> the teachings of the Buddha.
> Central to these teachings are the

concepts of truth, righteousness
and loving kindness. It is govern-
ment based on these very quali-
ties that the people of Burma
are seeking in their struggle for
democracy.[38]

Ride on King Jesus!
No man can hinder me
Ride on King Jesus!
No man can hinder me

I was a young child when folks at our church
were deeply involved in some painful strug-
gles related to the desegregation of the public
schools. A boycott of children from the schools
was looming over the horizon of the nego-
tiations. Clergy leaders faced the prospect of
arrest for violation of the law. When the day of
the boycott came, instead of going to our usual
school, we went to one of the Freedom Schools
being held in churches throughout the community. I do not really remember much of the
day, except my disappointment that I still had
to go to school. I had hoped that the freedom

---

38. 1991 Nobel Peace Prize presentation speech by Frances Sejersted for
Aung San Suu Kyi, www.nobelprize.org.

struggle might mean a day off. That was not to be. While it was Harriet Tubman we learned about instead of George Washington, it was still school, as far as a little boy was concerned.

But one other thing stands out in my memory. We learned a song, a spiritual composed and sung by the slaves, which has stayed with me till this day.

> *Ride on King Jesus!*
> *No man can hinder me*
> *Ride on King Jesus!*
> *No man can hinder me*

Looking back now I am very much aware that there was great wisdom in teaching us that spiritual in Freedom School.

Any who would seek any change for the good, usually against the odds, will need strength and wisdom greater than their own individually or collectively. Whether it is for the equality of all human beings, the righting of old wrongs, the rearrangement of unjust institutional structures, or action to end the harm being done by us to the very creation itself, any struggle for the good, the kind, the just, the loving, will be against seemingly intractable odds. So any who would seek human betterment, whether the improvement of the self, or the transformation of the world from the nightmare it often can be into something akin to the dream that God intends, will only likely do so over the long haul by a daring, courageous, conviction. And that conviction will ultimately be grounded in faith: faith that the universe is not governed by blind chance or enslaving fates; faith, that though the struggle may be long and costly, in the end, love wins, in the end, good will out, in the end, justice, in the end, mercy, in the end, the good.

Another old favorite hymn of my grandmother's comes to mind:

> O, for a faith that will not shrink,
> Though pressed by every foe,
> That will not tremble on the brink
> Of any earthly woe.[39]

It is not an accident that Aung San Suu Kyi and Malala Yousafzai affirmed this kind of enduring faith from their traditions. In fact, it is rather fascinating to read the Nobel lectures or the presentation speeches about

---

39. "O, For a Faith That Will Not Shrink," words by William H. Bathurst, 1831, www.cyberhymnal.org/htm/o/f/o4afaith.htm.

Desmond Tutu, Eli Weisel, the imprisoned anti-Nazi pacifist Carl von Ossietzky, the Dalai Lama, and the countless others. Their kind of faith, articulated in various ways and through the voice of differing traditions, seems to be a constant among all who have labored to change the world for the good. It was just such a faith that I suspect they were seeking to inculcate in us in Freedom School that day.

> *Ride on King Jesus!*
> *No man can hinder me*
> *Ride on King Jesus!*
> *No man can hinder me*

For the composer/singer of this old spiritual, Jesus embodied the fullness of the love, the goodness, the justice, the forgiveness, the grace, the Spirit, the reality of the living God. The language of Jesus riding on to victory, clearly through a great seismic struggle with the hosts of evil, was a poetic and prophetic way of talking about the ultimate victory of God, the triumphant reign of love, and the destined rule of goodness, of justice, and mercy. The singer perceived in the entrance of Jesus into the city of Jerusalem on that first Palm Sunday—that the victory of God, the victory of the good, the triumph of love, the resurrection of Jesus from the tyranny of death—was assured against all evidence to the contrary.

Think about the story of that Palm Sunday for a moment. Jesus didn't just happen to be in Jerusalem that day. His entrance had all of the marks of planning, coordination, intentionality, and skillful execution. Matthew, Mark and Luke all say that before he entered the holy city Jesus told several of his disciples to go get a donkey for him to ride. He then says that if anyone asks, "Why are you untying it? Just say this: 'The Lord needs it'" (Luke 19:31). And that is what happened. They enter the nearest village, find the donkey, untie and start to take it. Someone asked what they were doing taking it and they respond, "The Lord needs it." The people let them have it. Now, I do not suggest you try that with someone's Lexus in uptown Charlotte. What is going on here is that arrangements had been made for the donkey. This was planned. Jesus didn't just happen to ride into Jerusalem on Palm Sunday.

Think about the timing. It was the beginning of the Passover holy days. Jesus didn't just happen to be there at that time, either. The Passover was a celebration of freedom.

> Go down, Moses,
> way down in Egypt land,
> and tell old Pharaoh,
> let my people go.

A few years back I read *The Last Week: A Day by Day Account of Jesus's Final Week in Jerusalem*, by Marcus J. Borg and John Dominic Crossan. The book opened my eyes to the backstory of Holy Week, especially as grounded in Mark's Gospel, in ways nothing else had before or has since. Borg and Crossan describe in detail a background that reveals Jesus's careful prophetic planning and deeper evangelical intent.

Passover was about freedom. The feast of the Passover was, therefore, a dangerous occasion. It dared to declare the freedom of God in the midst of the tyranny of the empire—not the empire of ancient Egypt, but the empire of Rome. Jesus didn't just happen to be in Jerusalem around the feast of the Passover, the feast of God's freedom, and therefore ours. He knew what he was doing. Passover was a perfect time to strike a blow for freedom, to make protest against injustice and oppression. Even the Romans knew that.

That is why, as Borg and Crossan recall, Pontius Pilate, the Roman governor of Judea,

Idumea, and Samaria, left his palace at Fortress Antonia by the sea, arrogantly and disdainfully entering the city of Jerusalem through the western gate. He was on horseback, leading a Roman company of cavalry and infantry with the standards and insignia of the empire on vivid display. One can imagine insignia honoring the emperor bearing words like Caesar, Son of God, as Emperors of the Empire were often titled. The import of such words as Son of God applied to the rulers of Rome suggests the revolution implied in the Lordship, the Kingship of Jesus.

> We believe in one Lord, Jesus Christ . . . .
> God from God,
> Light from Light
> True God from true God . . .
> on the third day he rose again
>
> *Ride on King Jesus!*
> *No man can hinder me*
> *Ride on King Jesus!*
> *No man can hinder me*

Here Borg and Crossan note the extraordinary back story. It was while Pontius Pilate was entering the city from the western gate that

Jesus entered the city on the eastern side by the Mount of Olives. It was not an accident. Jesus didn't just happen to be there. Jesus knew what he was doing. Pilate entered on a war horse, which was the world's way. Jesus entered on a donkey. In doing this Jesus was skillfully sending a signal and message. There is another way and Jesus came to show it.

Listen to what the prophet wrote:

> Rejoice greatly, O daughter of Zion! Shout aloud, O daughter Jerusalem! Lo, your king comes to you; triumphant and victorious is he, humble and riding on a donkey, on a colt, the foal of a donkey. He shall cut off the chariot from Ephraim and the war horse from Jerusalem; and the battle bow shall be cut off, and he shall command peace to the nations; his dominion shall be from sea to sea, and from the River to the ends of the earth.

There is another way.

Blessed are the poor and the poor in spirit, he taught us. There is another way. Blessed are the meek. Blessed are the merciful, the compassionate. Blessed are you who hunger and thirst and labor that God's righteousness and justice might prevail. Blessed are the peacemakers. There is another way.

Love your enemies, bless those who curse you, pray for those who despitefully use you. There is another way.

Hear, O Israel, you shall love the Lord your God with all your heart all your soul and all your mind. And you shall love your neighbor as yourself. There is another way.

My house shall be called a house of prayer for all people, he taught us. There is another way.

Father, forgive them for they know not what they do, he said. Desmond Tutu is right, there is no future without forgiveness. There is another way.

It is not an easy way. Jesus called it the "narrow way." But it is the way. Don't give up. Don't give in. The very life and sanity of the world is at stake. Don't give up. Don't give in. There is a God. "He's still on the throne." And as one old song says, "He's got the whole world in his hands." If that is true the future can be faced, no matter how hard, no matter how uncertain, no matter how perplexing. That is the affirmation the singer was talking about. That is the faith that can face any future. That

is the conviction that will change our worlds
and can change the world.

> *Ride on King Jesus!*
> *No man can hinder me*
> *Ride on King Jesus!*
> *No man can hinder me*

CHAPTER 9

How to Know When the Spirit is in Your Church

O Lord my God, When I in awesome
  wonder,
Consider all the worlds Thy Hands
  have made;
I see the stars, I hear the rolling
  thunder,

Thy power throughout the universe displayed.

Then sings my soul, My Savior God, to Thee,
How great Thou art, How great Thou art.
Then sings my soul, My Savior God, to Thee,
How great Thou art, How great Thou art![40]

In the beginning when God created the heavens and the earth, the earth was a formless void and darkness covered the face of the deep, while a wind from God swept over the face of the waters. Then God said, "Let there be light"; and there was light. (Genesis 1:1–2)

And God stepped out on space and said, I'm lonely, I'll make me a world.
(A Slave Preacher, *God's Trombones*)

---

40. *LEVAS II*, #60.

Jurgen Moltmann is appropriately well-known and respected for his theology of hope. He inspired many who sought a theology that was at once faithful and orthodox, and therefore passionately committed to the making of a more loving, just, and humane world reflecting the teachings and the way of Jesus. In a book on God's creation he said: "God does not create merely by calling something into existence, or by setting something afoot. In a more profound sense he creates by letting be, by making room, and by withdrawing himself."[41]

When God steps out, look out: a new world's about to be made! When God created the world it was as though "the Great God Almighty" moved over, if you will, and made room and space for the other: for something or someone other than God's own self. When God said, "Let there be," God, in effect, limited himself in order to make space for the other, the created reality of that which is, living and non-living, *visible and invisible*, as the Nicene Creed says.

---

41. Jurgen Moltmann, *God in Creation: A New Theology of Creation and the Spirit of God* (Minneapolis: Fortress Press, 1993), 88.

Long before Moltmann composed his theology, an old slave preacher spinning the poetry of new possibility that we call preaching, grasped this and made it the edge of hope. James Weldon Johnson in his poetic anthology, *God's Trombones*, recreates the sermons of these slave preacher-poet-prophets of antebellum America. The poems are masterpieces of wisdom, pathos, and spiritual energy. The story of the Bible connects with the story of life being lived and from that conjunction of the story of our lives with the biblical story, new life becomes a real possibility. And through these poems you can hear those strange and not-too-distant voices of old slave preachers telling the Bible story into contemporary life.

One of the preaching poems, "Go down, death," dares to face death. One, "The Crucifixion," re-tells the steps of Jesus carrying the cross. When Jesus is being crucified, when hands that only healed and helped are being themselves hurt and harmed by nails pinning them to a dying tree, the poem says it all simply: "the hammer, the hammer, the hammer." These are poems of incredible pathos and power born of the creative conjunction of the Word of God and the lives of the preacher and people, enslaved by the world but being set free by the Word.

The best known of these poems is probably "The Creation." It begins with these words:

> And God stepped out on space,
> And he looked around and said:
> "I'm lonely—
> I'll make me a world."[42]

Though untutored and unlettered, these preacher-prophets were poets. By the Spirit and a genius deep within the soul of their experience of God, they grasped the power of words to say more than mere words ever could. This preaching is poetry.

The job of poetry is to stretch language beyond its limits, pointing us beyond the limitations of what is, to the limitless possibilities of what can be. The point of poetry is to point not to itself, but to what Bonhoeffer called "the beyond in our midst," to the profound depth

---

42. James Weldon Johnson, "The Creation," in *The Book of American Negro Poetry*, ed. James Weldon Johnson (1922; New York: BiblioBazaar, 2006). 94.

of life, to its transcendent height, to "the hope of glory." Poetry points beyond the limits of "reality" to the limitlessness of "mystery" that is the ultimate depth and the height of reality. This is poetry that seeks to point to the ultimate mystery of our creation. Just listen to the language. "And God stepped out on space." How do you step out on space? This is clearly pointing us to something mere prose cannot reach. But if you look at the biblical story of creation the poet has gotten hold of something.

There are just some realities that are so incredible, so deep, so awesome that you can only point to them. You cannot take hold and control them. I remember in college reading an essay Sigmund Freud wrote on happiness. I am sure it accurately described the psychological and scientific dimensions of happiness. But when I finished reading it, I was depressed. There are just some things so deep, so awesome, so incredible, so filled with mystery that language falls short. Prose cannot get it. The didactic cannot get it. The literal just does not get it. There are limitations to the literal. Sometimes you have to find a metaphor. Sometimes you have to compose a poem. Sometimes you have to dance a dance or sing a song. There is an African proverb that says that "without a song the gods will not descend."

The ultimate mystery of creation defies the limits of our language. The old slave preachers grasped this.

> And God stepped out on space,
> And he looked around and said:
> "I'm lonely—
> I'll make me a world."

When God steps out, look out: a new world's about to be made!

The aloneness of which the preacher speaks, of course, is not some neurotic need of God being worked out in creation. Part of what the doctrine of the Holy Trinity teaches us is that the God who is One God embraces within that Oneness both unity and diversity, singularity and plurality, individuality and community. Augustine was right when he taught us that the Triune God is a community of love. The aloneness of which the teacher speaks is not neurotic. God is God. The insight is that it is the very nature of who God is to create space for the other to be and to grow.

And God stepped out on space,
And he looked around and said:
"I'm lonely—
I'll make me a world."

When God steps out, look out: a new world's about to be made!

Creation was made for communion and relationship. To put it another way, we were made for God and each other. That is what the story of Adam and Eve in the Garden of Eden in Genesis 2 and 3 is saying. As long as Adam and Eve are in communion and relationship with God and each other, they are in paradise. And when that communion and relationship is fractured or broken, John Milton's prophetic poetry becomes painfully true: paradise is lost. We were made for God and each other.

We were made for loving relationship and intimacy with the God who created us and with each other as children of that one God and Creator of us all. I suspect that is why, when pressed, Jesus declared that the entire religious and spiritual enterprise, the entire purpose of life itself, the secret and the reason for our being, and the way our being becomes a life worth living may be found in these two truths: "'You shall love the Lord your God with all your heart, and with all your soul, and with all your mind.' This is the greatest and first commandment. And a second is like it: 'You shall love your neighbor as yourself.' On these two commandments hang all the law and the prophets" (Matthew 22:37–40).

My grandmother, as most members of my family on both sides, was a dyed-in-the-wool, rock-ribbed Baptist. She actually had a remarkable openness to the ways of God, and in her spirit anticipated not only ecumenical openness, but interfaith openness to all people. When I was in junior high school my mother died of a massive cerebral hemorrhage, probably caused by damage sustained from a childhood head trauma when she was accidentally hit by a car. For nearly a year she was in a coma until she eventually died. Health insurance only covered the hospitalization and related medical care. After the hospitalization she was in a nursing home. Insurance did not pay for that. My father worked two jobs to make ends meet. The expense nearly broke us financially.

The bishop and the clergy of our diocese in Western New York helped out with some of the expenses. People in our home parish helped out by allowing Daddy to work both as their priest and to teach in public school. Often, when necessary, church folk would keep my sister and me. My cousin Billy moved in and helped. Grandma moved and helped. Looking back it was an incredible act of community that sustained us during the crisis of her coma and eventual death. Grandma and Daddy became particularly close during this time. They would tease and joke with each other quite regularly.

When my mother was eventually placed in a nursing home we would usually visit in the evening after school. We would sometimes do homework, watch television, and do what we would have done at home in the family room. When it was time to leave, either Grandma or Daddy would pray. The family joke was that Daddy's prayers (usually from the Book of Common Prayer) were always short and to the point. Grandma's were another story. Daddy used to tease her saying that. "The poor Lord probably falls asleep listening to you pray for everything and everybody."

Every once and a while Grandma would joke with Daddy about the Episcopal Church. She actually had a deep reverence for any way that leads to God. One time there was a tent revival held near our house. We kids went to see the folk "get happy" and "fall out." We really enjoyed it. When we got home Grandma found out and questioned us. When we had spilled our guts, she said very simply, "Don't ever laugh at other people's religion. God made us all different. You respect that."

My passion as a follower of Jesus for social justice and equal rights for all people is born not of a social theory but from her words: "God made us all different. You respect that." God made us. And God made us all different. There was a world in what she said. God made us. God is our Creator. God is "our Father" in heaven. God is our "Mother" who comforts us as a "mother comforts" her child (Isaiah 66:13). God made us.

The prophet Malachi prefaced his call for justice and fair treatment of everyone with these words: "Have we not all one father? Has not one God created us?" (Malachi 2:10). We are equally children of the one God and Father of us all, and meant to be treated as such. Our divine creation confers dignity, value, worth, and equality and that has implications for how we relate to each other personally and politically, locally, nationally, globally.

God made us. And God made us different. There must be room equally for all because that is how God made us. Justice must be applied equally, because God made us all. No child was born to lack education or food because God made us all and we are equally all his children. God made us. And God made us different. An old Latin hymn says it this way:

> Where charity and love prevail
> here God is ever found;
> Brought here together by Christ's love
> By love we thus are bound.
>
> Love can exclude no race or creed
> If honored be God's name;
> Our common life embraces all
> Whose Father is the same. [43]

I didn't know it at the time but I was learning about real nitty-gritty faith, born of a very real God, lived with humor and hope mixed amidst the sadness and hardship. It was a spirituality and theology of hope, even when walking through hell. Periodically during the banter between Grandma and Daddy about religion— a frequent topic—she would ask, with a smile on her face and twinkle in her eye: "How do you know when the Spirit is in your church?

43. *The Hymnal 1982*, 581.

Nobody shouts. Nobody really sings. Nothing happens? How do you know?"

When my mother, her daughter, died, we were, as we had been for the long journey of her illness, surrounded by that same community of love, family, friends, church folk. During the meal after the burial, when everyone seemed to be in the same place at the same time, Grandma leaned over to Daddy and said, "When you are loved like this you can bet the Spirit is somewhere around."

Another old Latin hymn confirms:

> God is love,
> and where true love is
> God himself is there.[44]

Such love creates the space where "the beloved community" can happen. Indeed, it was just such love that moved God to move over and to make room and space for the world. Jurgen Moltmann said it this way,

> God withdraws himself from
> himself to himself in order to

---

44. *The Hymnal 1982*, 577.

> make creation possible. His cre-
> ative activity outwards is pre-
> ceded by his humble divine self
> restriction. . . . God's creative love
> is grounded in his humble, self-
> humiliating love. . . . God does
> not create by merely calling some-
> thing into existence, or by set-
> ting something afoot. In a more
> profound sense he creates by
> letting-be, by making room, and
> by withdrawing himself."[45]

It is this "self-humiliating love" which makes room and space for others which is a sure and certain sign of the movement of the Spirit of the living God.

How do you know when the Spirit is in your church? Another old song says it this way:

> There's a sweet, sweet Spirit in this
>   place
> And I know it is the Spirit of the
>   Lord.
> Sweet Holy Spirit,
> Sweet heavenly dove

---

45. Jurgen Moltmann, *God in Creation*, 88.

Stay right here with us,
Filling us with your love
And for these blessings,
We lift our hearts in praise.
Without a doubt we'll know
That we have been revived,
When we shall leave this place."[46]

Stay right here with us.

---

46. *LEVAS II*, #120.

CHAPTER 10

Who'll Be a Witness?

My soul is a witness for my Lord
My soul is a witness for my Lord
My soul is a witness for my Lord
My soul is a witness for my Lord

You read in the Bible and you
   understand
Metuselah was the oldest man
He lived nine hundred and ninety
   nine
He died and went to Heav'n, Lord,
   in a-due time

Metuselah was a witness for my Lord
Metuselah was a witness for my Lord
Metuselah was a witness for my Lord
Metuselah was a witness for my Lord

O, who'll be a witness for my Lord
Who'll be a witness for my Lord
My soul is a witness for my Lord
My soul is a witness for my Lord[47]

The message of the spiritual "Witness for My Lord" may well be found in the internal structure and logic as much as in the lyrics and the music. It begins simply enough: "My soul is a witness for my Lord." The successive stanzas and verses of the song build on that first one, telling the stories of biblical people whose lives made a witness. It begins with Methuselah who is mentioned in Genesis has having lived a long time and reminds us "Methuselah was a witness for my Lord." It goes on and tells the story of other folks. Like the music of improvised jazz or the lyrics of improvised rap, the stories of biblical people who witnessed can be added to the song, each with the refrain declaring that they were "a witness for my Lord."

---

47. www.negrospirituals.com/songs/witness_for_my_lord.htm.

> Now Samson was a witness for my
>   Lord
> Deborah was a witness for my Lord.
> Esther, Daniel, Mary, Paul . . . .

Then, after going through the biblical story, the singer comes to the last verse and asks "Now who will be a witness for my Lord?" Moving from the biblical past to a new biblical present, the singer makes the bold affirmation, "My soul is a witness for my Lord."

> O, who'll be a witness for my Lord
> Who'll be a witness for my Lord
> My soul is a witness for my Lord
> My soul is a witness for my Lord
>
> Who will be a witness for my Lord?

A few years ago, when I first went on Facebook, I filled out the information section that was part of the process of setting up a page. I answered the questions with some ease, mindful of not giving addresses and phone numbers. Then I came to a question that stumped me. It asked for my religious affiliation. I was just about to answer with ease by inserting the word "Christian," but I hesitated, not because I was having a religious identity crisis, or because I would rather be a closet Christian. Hardly. I became aware in that moment that my answer was about to spin out there into cyber-orbit. People could read into that answer all sorts of things that I never intended and that gave me pause.

It seems to me that in many respects the word "Christian" has been hijacked to mean things that do not have much of anything to do with Jesus. Far too often in popular culture the word "Christian" has come to mean fundamentalist, narrow-minded, bigoted, anti-intellectual, homophobic, misogynist, and on and on and on. Faith is not about liberal or conservative leanings but about following the way of Jesus rather than capitulating to currents of cultural Christianity. We need some witnesses to a way of being Christian that looks something like Jesus.

The Jesus who said,

> The Spirit of the Lord is upon me,
> because he has anointed me
> to bring good news to the poor.
> He has sent me to proclaim release
> to the captives
> and recovery of sight to the blind,
> to let the oppressed go free,

to proclaim the year of the Lord's
favor.

The Jesus who said, "By this everyone will
know that you are my disciples, if you have
love for one another" (John 13:35).

The Jesus who said, "'Hear, O Israel: the
Lord our God, the Lord is one; you shall love the
Lord your God with all your heart, and with all
your soul, and with all your mind, and with all
your strength.' The second [commandment] is
this, 'You shall love your neighbor as yourself.'
There is no other commandment greater than
these" (Mark 12:29–31).

We need witnesses to a Christianity that
looks something like Jesus of Nazareth. We
need some witnesses to the love of God that
we have seen in the face of Jesus because witnesses like that will change the world. Bishop
Mark Hollingsworth and the good people of the
Diocese of Ohio coined a slogan based on the
teaching of Jesus about loving God and loving
our neighbor that says:

Love God.
Love your neighbor.
Change the world!

That is it. Witness to the way of love changes the witness, changes those who witness the witness, and changes the world in which the witness is made.

> Love God.
> Love your neighbor.
> Change the world!

As much as my grandmother loved church and went to church, my grandfather rarely set foot in the place. He did not trust preachers particularly, though he liked my father, who was one. He was highly opinionated and had firm social and political opinions. He was a Republican because of Lincoln. He was always suspicious of Democrats though John Kennedy began to change that. But he was not high on church. I suspect there were some stories I never asked, but I do remember him arguing that churches promised folks heaven, took their money, and then went to the bank. As far as I can remember Grandpa never went to church except for funerals, though he kept and read his Bible and said his prayers every night, getting down on his knees. I remember that because my sister Sharon, my cousin Ronald, and I would sometimes sneak into his room while he was saying his prayers and tickle his feet.

In a strange way, grandpa did have a church. It was Ebbets field. His denomination, the Brooklyn Dodgers. The pastor and deacon, Jackie Robinson and Branch Rickey. So when the film *42* came out, telling the story of Jackie Robinson and the desegregation of major league baseball, my wife and I were among the first in line to see it. There is a part of me that would like to require watching *42* as part of preparation for Holy Baptism and Confirmation.

In the first half of the twentieth century baseball had become "America's Game," if you will, and like America at that time baseball was racially segregated. There were the classic old Negro Leagues for black players and the American and National Leagues for white players, and the twain never met until Number 42, until Jackie Robinson.

The engineer behind breaking the color barrier was a man named Branch Rickey, the General Manager of the old Brooklyn Dodgers. Rickey was a tough old ball player and businessman. He drank bourbon, smoked cigars, cursed like a sailor, and he loved Jesus. He was a devout Christian who tried to live out the deeper spirit of the question "what would Jesus do" in his own life as a businessman who loved baseball. It was precisely because he loved baseball that he refused to allow baseball to remain bigoted and segregated.

Real love is not soft, sweet, and sentimental. Real love seeks what is truly good and just and kind and compassionate, even if it is counter-cultural and contrary to the unenlightened self-interest of the status quo. Branch Rickey loved baseball enough to work to change it. The film tells the story of how Rickey went about doing this and the extraordinary role and sacrifice of Jackie Robinson in making it happen. There are some great moments in the movie, because Rickey really was a character. As I watched it the first time I kept thinking that the person who played Rickey looked familiar, but I couldn't quite place him. Then at some point I recognized him. It was Harrison Ford. He had so become the character of Rickey that he was almost unrecognizable as himself.

When Branch Rickey and his staff were trying to identify a player from the Negro League to bring up, they eventually chose Robinson. There were other players with better stats and who might have been better on the field, but Rickey made up his mind that he wanted Robinson. Rickey knew that whoever the ballplayer was, he would have to be a player of extraordinary professional excellence on the field and a person of spiritual excellence in his soul. Rickey saw in Robinson both capacities, a great ballplayer and a great soul.

Rickey's advisors were not convinced. But after Rickey had made up his mind, he did something familiar to almost all parents: he ended the discussion essentially saying, "because I said so." When one of his advisors asked him one last time, "Why do you want Robinson?" He answered: "Because I'm a Methodist, Robinson is a Methodist, and God is a Methodist." Decision made. End of discussion.

The film did not portray an exchange that occurred between Rickey and Robinson when they first met. At one point in the conversation Rickey took out a little book by Giovanni Papini, titled *Life of Christ* and read passages about the teachings of Jesus in the Sermon on the Mount.

> Blessed are the poor and the poor in spirit.
> Blessed are the merciful, the compassionate.
> Blessed are those who hunger and thirst that God's righteous justice might prevail.

Blessed are the peacemakers.
Blessed are you when you are
  persecuted for the cause of right.

Do unto other as you would have
  them do unto you.

Love your enemies.
Bless those who curse you.
Pray for those who despitefully use
  you.

After the reading Robinson agreed. They shook hands and these two people, daring to live the teaching of Jesus about the way of love, daring to witness to the power of that love, changed baseball. And baseball helped to change America. The witness to human equality, dignity, and freedom helped to change the world from the nightmare it often was into something closer to the dream of God for all.

O, who'll be a witness for my Lord
Who'll be a witness for my Lord
My soul is a witness for my Lord
My soul is a witness for my Lord

CHAPTER   11

Keep Going!

Walk together children
Don' you get weary
Walk together children
Don't you get weary
Oh, walk together children
Don't you get weary
There's a great camp meeting in the
    promised land[48]

48.www.negrospirituals.com/songs/walk_together_children.
htm.

124

> Once while Jesus was standing
> beside the lake of Gennesaret, and
> the crowd was pressing in on him
> to hear the word of God, he saw
> two boats there at the shore of the
> lake; the fishermen had gone out of
> them and were washing their nets.
> He got into one of the boats, the
> one belonging to Simon, and asked
> him to put out a little way from the
> shore. Then he sat down and taught
> the crowds from the boat. When
> he had finished speaking, he said
> to Simon, "Put out into the deep
> water and let down your nets for a
> catch." Simon answered, "Master,
> we have worked all night long but
> have caught nothing. Yet if you say
> so, I will let down the nets." When
> they had done this, they caught
> so many fish that their nets were
> beginning to break. (Luke 5:1–6)

I never actually saw the Hollywood movie *Son
of God*, so I am not commending it to you, but
I saw the trailer for it and it was really good.
It shows a scene near the beginning of Jesus's

ministry. The director has combined several stories in the Gospels here, but the interpretation of the message is right on. Jesus is in a fishing boat with Peter. Peter is frustrated. The fish are not biting. The nets are not catching any fish and the economy of first century Galilee depended on the fishing industry at the Sea of Galilee. Peter's livelihood depended on it. People needed the fish to eat. Peter's frustration may have represented the frustration of people who are working more and making less. It may have represented the frustration of an economy that may never again be what it was.

Here's where Hollywood comes in. As in the biblical text above, Jesus senses Peter's frustration and tells him to put his net into the deep water. Peter shrugs as if to say, "Whatever," but he does as Jesus tells him. He casts the net out into the deep. The camera then goes underwater, looking up toward the surface. You can see the face of Jesus reflected through the ripples of the water. Then Jesus touches the water and there is commotion and a troubling of the waters. In the next scene, the camera is back up on the surface, and you see Peter now struggling with others to pull in the nets that are filled with fish. After they have hauled in the fish, Jesus says to Peter: "Now come and follow me." You can imagine Peter thinking, *What? The fish are biting, and you want to go somewhere else?* Instead, Peter says, "Where are we going?" Jesus responds, "To change the world."

God came into the world to change the world from the nightmare it often is into the dream that God intends. God did not come into the world to leave it the way God found it. God came to change it, to change us, to change our society, to change our global community, and to show us the way of transformation, the way of new life, the way of the reign and kingdom of God in our midst.

Author Max Lucado once wrote, "God loves you just the way you are, but he does not intend to leave you that way." God so loved the world, as John 3:16 says, that God came to the world. God came to show the way into God's dream. We who have accepted baptism in the way of Jesus have joined the movement that follows the way of Jesus from nightmare to dream.

Some years ago the late South African Dominican priest Albert Nolan reminded us that God didn't come into the world in the Person of Jesus of Nazareth to establish an institution, or even to found a religion. Jesus inaugurated a movement, the Way, as the New Testament called it, the Way of transformation—new birth, new creation—the Way into what the late Verna Dozier called the dream that God intends. Jesus came as the leader of a movement to share in God's mission of liberating love.

Think about it for a moment. Jesus never asked anybody to join his church or his group. He didn't hand out pew cards saying, "If you do not have a church home, consider ours." Instead, Jesus invited people into the moment of his movement, his movement of the Way. Baptism was not admission into a club, but initiation into this movement, this Way, this community of the Way, the Way of Jesus. The Church exists to serve the movement, not the other way around. We are the Body of Christ in the Episcopal way of following Jesus. It will be only as we reclaim and recover the deeper sense of being part of the Jesus movement, the movement of the Spirit in the world today, that we will find our life anew in this mission moment in which we live. We are part of the Jesus movement to change the world from a nightmare into God's dream. If you do not believe me, ask Jesus.

Follow me, he says. We are a movement.

Follow me and I will make you fish for people.
We are a movement.

*Follow me and I will make you more than you
ever dreamed you could be.* We are a movement.

Follow me and I will show you the way of
love, which is the only way.

Follow me and I will show you how to be
born again and how to build the new creation.

Follow me and I will show you the way of
transformation.

Follow me and I will show you a life of dignity, a life of integrity, a life of vitality, a life
saturated with eternity.

Follow me and I will show you a life that
not even the titanic powers of death, hell, judgment, and evil can ever take away.

Follow me and I will show you how to be
changed, how to change the world, how to be
born again, how to build the new creation.

Follow me and I will show you how to
change the world.

Follow me. We are a movement.

Follow me and change the world!

Maybe a patron saint for us, the body of
Christ, the Church in our time, is a woman
many in her time called "Moses." You know
her. I am talking about Harriet Tubman.

Born into chattel slavery, she was baptized in an Episcopal Church. But she was not baptized into slavery. She was baptized into Christ, into the movement called the Way, and that Way that she joined and followed so faithfully and fearlessly, can change the world. As Paul says in Galatians,

> As many of you as were baptized into Christ have clothed yourselves with Christ. There is no longer Jew or Greek, there is no longer slave or free, there is no longer male and female; for all of you are one in Christ Jesus. (Galatians 3:27, 28)

Harriet Tubman was a leader in the Underground Railroad, part of the nineteenth century movement that was committed to the abolition of slavery. People called her "Moses" because on about twenty pilgrimages into American slave territory, she led some three hundred former slaves through "the danger waters" to freedom. She would often say that she just went where the Spirit said to go, like Joan of Arc. Harriet Tubman was a person who saw her visions, and followed the Spirit.

If you hear the dogs, keep going.
If you see the torches in the woods, keep going.
If there's shouting after you, keep going.
Don't ever stop. Don't ever quit.
Don't give up. Don't give in.
If you want a taste of freedom,
Keep going!